Life in the Colonies

TEACHER RESOURCES
GRADE 5 • UNIT 4

4

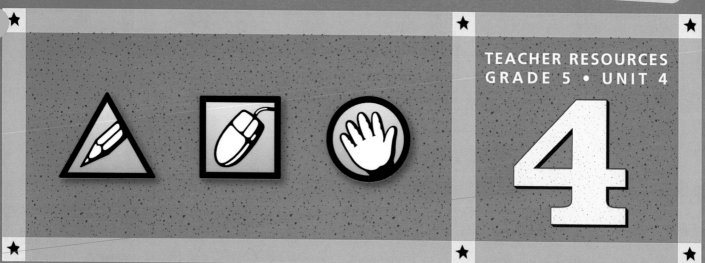

HISTORY-SOCIAL SCIENCE FOR CALIFORNIA
OUR NATION

H-SS 5.4 Students understand the political, religious, social, and economic institutions that evolved in the colonial era.

LESSON 1 5.4.1 Understand the influence of location and physical setting on the founding of the original 13 colonies, and identify on a map the locations of the colonies and of the American Indian nations already inhabiting these areas.

LESSON 2 5.4.2 Identify the major individuals and groups responsible for the founding of the various colonies and the reasons for their founding (e.g., John Smith, Virginia; Roger Williams, Rhode Island; William Penn, Pennsylvania; Lord Baltimore, Maryland; William Bradford, Plymouth; John Winthrop, Massachusetts).

LESSON 3 5.4.3 Describe the religious aspects of the earliest colonies (e.g., Puritanism in Massachusetts, Anglicanism in Virginia, Catholicism in Maryland, Quakerism in Pennsylvania).

LESSON 4 5.4.4 Identify the significance and leaders of the First Great Awakening, which marked a shift in religious ideas, practices, and allegiances in the colonial period, the growth of religious toleration, and free exercise of religion.

LESSON 5 5.4.5 Understand how the British colonial period created the basis for the development of political self-government and a free-market economic system and the differences between the British, Spanish, and French colonial systems.

LESSON 6 5.4.6 Describe the introduction of slavery into America, the responses of slave families to their condition, the ongoing struggle between proponents and opponents of slavery, and the gradual institutionalization of slavery in the South.

LESSON 7 5.4.7 Explain the early democratic ideas and practices that emerged during the colonial period, including the significance of representative assemblies and town meetings.

Editorial Offices: Glenview, Illinois • Parsippany, New Jersey • New York, New York

Sales Offices: Needham, Massachusetts • Duluth, Georgia • Glenview, Illinois
Coppell, Texas • Sacramento, California • Mesa, Arizona

ISBN: 0-328-15516-0

Grade 5
Unit 4 — Life in the Colonies
Contents

Quick Planner	**65**T2
Unit Materials	**65**T5
English-Language Arts Guide	**65**T6
Study Journal	**65**
Unit Project	**66**T2

Lessons

Lesson 1
What influenced where Europeans settled in North America? **67**T2

Lesson 2
Who founded the colonies and why? **71**T2

Lesson 3
How did religion affect the founding of the colonies? **77**T2

Lesson 4
How did the First Great Awakening affect the colonies? **81**T2

Lesson 5
What systems developed in the colonies? **85**T2

Lesson 6
What was the role of slavery in colonial America? **89**T2

Lesson 7
What brought on democratic ideas in colonial America? **93**T2

Resources **96**T9

Teacher:

Copy this planner.

Core Instruction: △ Text Path

Alternate Instruction: ☐ Digital Path ◯ Active Path

Content Paths

English-Language Arts Support

Lesson 1

H-SS 5.4.1 Understand the influence of location and physical setting on the founding of the original 13 colonies, and identify on a map the locations of the colonies and of the American Indian nations already inhabiting these areas.

What influenced where Europeans settled in North America?

△ Text Path, pp. **67**T4, **67–70**
35 min. **Skill: Resource Maps**

☐ Digital Path, p. **70**T1
50 min. **Video: The Thirteen Colonies**

◯ Active Path, pp. **70**T2–T4
50 min. **Activity: Character Cards**

Reading Transparency, **R** 14

Reading Comprehension Skill
⦿ Make Generalizations
ELA 5RC2.4

Vocabulary Development
Root Words
ELA 5RW1.2

Lesson 2

H-SS 5.4.2 Identify the major individuals and groups responsible for the founding of the various colonies and the reasons for their founding (e.g., John Smith, Virginia; Roger Williams, Rhode Island; William Penn, Pennsylvania; Lord Baltimore, Maryland; William Bradford, Plymouth; John Winthrop, Massachusetts).

Who founded the colonies and why?

△ Text Path, pp. **71**T4, **71–76**
50 min. **Skill: Classifying and Sorting**

☐ Digital Path, p. **76**T1
50 min. **Video: Founding the Colonies**

◯ Active Path, pp. **76**T2–T4
100 min. **Activity: Research Colonial Leaders**

Reading Transparency, **R** 15

Reading Comprehension Skill
Compare and Contrast
ELA 5RC2.1

Vocabulary Development
Root Words
ELA 5RW1.2

Lesson 3

H-SS 5.4.3 Describe the religious aspects of the earliest colonies (e.g., Puritanism in Massachusetts, Anglicanism in Virginia, Catholicism in Maryland, Quakerism in Pennsylvania).

Content Paths

How did religion affect the founding of the colonies?

△ Text Path, pp. **77**T4, **77–80**
35 min. **Biography: Anne Hutchinson**

☐ Digital Path, p. **80**T1
50 min. **Video: *Religion and the Colonies***

○ Active Path, pp. **80**T2–T4
50 min. **Activity: Examine Biographies**

English-Language Arts Support

Reading Transparency, **R**16

Reading Comprehension Skill
Make Generalizations

ELA 5RC2.4

Vocabulary Development
Prefixes

ELA 5RW1.4

Synonyms/Antonyms

ELA 5RW1.3

Lesson 4

H-SS 5.4.4 Identify the significance and leaders of the First Great Awakening, which marked a shift in religious ideas, practices, and allegiances in the colonial period, the growth of religious toleration, and free exercise of religion.

How did the First Great Awakening affect the colonies?

△ Text Path, pp. **81**T4, **81–84**
35 min. **Skill: Circle Graphs**

☐ Digital Path, p. **84**T1
50 min. **Video: *The First Great Awakening***

○ Active Path, pp. **84**T2–T4
100 min. **Activity: Primary Sources of the Great Awakening**

Reading Transparency, **R**17

Reading Comprehension Skill
Main Idea and Details

ELA 5RC2.3

Vocabulary Development
Suffixes

ELA 5RW1.4

Lesson 5

H-SS 5.4.5 Understand how the British colonial period created the basis for the development of political self-government and a free-market economic system and the differences between the British, Spanish, and French colonial systems.

What systems developed in the colonies?

△ Text Path, pp. **85**T4, **85–88**
35 min. **Citizenship: Rules of Civility**

☐ Digital Path, p. **88**T1
50 min. **Video: *Colonial Systems***

○ Active Path, pp. **88**T2–T4
50 min. **Activity: Situation Cards**

Reading Transparency, **R**18

Reading Comprehension Skill
Compare and Contrast

ELA 5RC2.1

Vocabulary Development
Related Words

ELA 5RW1.2

Content Paths

English-Language Arts Support

Lesson 6

H-SS 5.4.6 Describe the introduction of slavery into America, the responses of slave families to their condition, the ongoing struggle between proponents and opponents of slavery, and the gradual institutionalization of slavery in the South.

What was the role of slavery in colonial America?

△ 35 min. Text Path, pp. **89**T4, **89–92**
Primary Source: Autobiographies

□ 50 min. Digital Path, p. **92**T1
Video: Slavery in Colonial America

○ 100 min. Active Path, pp. **92**T2–T4
Activity: Analyzing Primary Sources

Reading Transparency, **R**19

Reading Comprehension Skill
Make Generalizations
ELA 5RC2.4

Vocabulary Development
Synonyms/Antonyms
ELA 5RW1.3

Lesson 7

H-SS 5.4.7 Explain the early democratic ideas and practices that emerged during the colonial period, including the significance of representative assemblies and town meetings.

What brought on democratic ideas in colonial America?

△ 35 min. Text Path, pp. **93**T4, **93–96**
Citizenship: Colonial and U.S. Governments

□ 50 min. Digital Path, p. **96**T1
Video: Colonial Democracies

○ 100 min. Active Path, pp. **96**T2–T4
Activity: Create a Colonial Government

Reading Transparency, **R**20

Reading Comprehension Skill
Make Generalizations
ELA 5RC2.4

Vocabulary Development
Root Words
ELA 5RW1.2

★ Assessment

(digital) **Lesson Pretest**

Ongoing Assessments, pp. 67T4, 70T1, 70T2; 71T4, 76T1, 76T2; 77T4, 80T1, 80T2; 81T4, 84T1, 84T2; 85T4, 88T1, 88T2; 89T4, 92T1, 92T2; 93T4, 96T1, 96T2

Lesson Assessments, pp. 70T6, 76T6, 80T6, 84T6, 88T6, 92T6, 96T6

(digital) **Lesson Quiz**

Culminating Writing, pp. 96T27–T30

Unit Multiple-Choice Test, pp. 96T31–T33

Unit Short-Answer Test, pp. 96T34–T36

(digital) **Benchmark Test**

Student Materials

Student Text, pp. 67–96

Content Readers, p. 96 T10

Jamestown

The Jamestown Colony

John Smith and the Survival of Jamestown

Time Line Card Masters, pp. 96 T15–T16

Vocabulary Card Masters, pp. 96 T17–T22

Biography Card Masters, pp. 96 T23–T26

Vocabulary & Biography Cards

Student & Big Book Atlases

Desk Map

Teacher Materials

Reading Transparencies, R 14–R 20

Writing Transparencies, W 7–W 8

Student Text Transparencies, pp. 67–96

Unit 4 Poster

Read-Aloud Literature, p. 96 T11

The Pilgrims of Plimoth by Marcia Sewall

School-to-Home Newsletter, pp. 96 T13–T14

Getting the Most from Your Materials

Vocabulary Card Masters, pp. 96 T17–T22

Pairing Game Play this game throughout Unit 4 to allow students to learn vocabulary.

1. Students, in pairs, take out their vocabulary cards. Player 1 spreads her cards on a desk or table, word side up. Player 2 spreads his cards on the same surface, definition side up.

2. Player 1 picks a word card. She finds the definition that matches the word and turns over the card. If the words match, she keeps the pair. If not, Player 2 gets a chance to match the same card.

3. If neither player matches the card, it is returned to its place on the desk. Players repeat the process until all cards are used or until time is up.

Unit Poster

Display the Unit 4 Poster. Have students describe the things they see in the poster.

Discuss the Unit Essential Question: "What people, ideas, and events shaped the development of the English colonies?" Ask: *What do you think you will learn about in this unit?* Write students' predictions on the board.

Revisit the poster and essential question throughout the unit. As students complete each lesson, have them write what they have learned on a piece of paper. Post the pieces of paper near or around the poster.

At the end of the unit, have students write a one-paragraph response that answers the Unit Essential Question.

Reading

Comprehension Skill:
◎ Make Generalizations

Readers use evidence in the text along with prior knowledge to make generalizations about commonalities among people, places, or events. Write the word *generalization* and the word *fact* on the board. Write these two sentences underneath: *Many families were self-sufficient. Timber from trees was used to build homes.* Remind students that a generalization makes a broad statement based on facts. Encourage students to look carefully at each sentence to decide which one is a fact and which is a generalization. Point out that writers often use clue words such as *many*, *most*, *all*, *sometimes*, *generally*, *always*, *never*, and *often* to signal generalizations. Use Transparencies **R**14, **R**16, **R**19, and **R**20 to teach this skill.

IF students are unable to identify generalizations,

THEN remind them to ask themselves: *Does this statement tell what many people, places, or events have in common?*

Vocabulary Development:
Root Words

Each Reading Transparency also has a vocabulary lesson that should be used to reinforce vocabulary development. Use Transparencies **R**14, **R**15, and **R**20 to model for students the skill of identifying root words. Readers gain meaning from content related terms by applying knowledge of known elements such as prefixes, suffixes, and root words to unfamiliar words. Write the following headings on the board: *prefix, root word, suffix*. Have students analyze the following words and identify the root word and affixes:

debtor	debt (something owed)	-or (somebody that does)
dissenter	dissent (not agree)	-er (somebody that does)
preacher	preach (giving sermon)	-er (one who does)
artisan	arti (visual, creating)	-an (a certain kind of person)

IF students have difficulty identifying root words and affixes,

THEN model a think-aloud strategy for finding known parts of words and applying word knowledge to determine meaning for each listed word.

Reading Support

Unit Skill
◎ Make Generalizations
Lessons 1, 3, 6, 7   ELA 5RC2.4
• Reading Transparencies, **R**14, **R**16, **R**19, **R**20
• Student Text, pp. **67, 77, 89, 93**
• Lesson Assessments, pp. **70**T6, **80**T6, **92**T6, **96**T6

Additional Skills
Compare and Contrast
Lessons 2, 5   ELA 5RC2.1

Main Idea and Details
Lesson 4   ELA 5RC2.3

Content Readers
p. **96**T10

Vocabulary Support

Unit Skill
Root Words
Lessons 1, 2, 7   ELA 5RW1.2
• Reading Transparencies, **R**14, **R**15, **R**20
• Student Text, pp. **67, 71, 93**

Additional Skills
Prefixes
Lesson 3   ELA 5RW1.4

Synonyms/Antonyms
Lessons 3, 6   ELA 5RW1.3

Suffixes
Lesson 4   ELA 5RW1.4

Related Words
Lesson 5   ELA 5RW1.3

Vocabulary Cards

Writing
Application Skill:
Write Narratives

Tell students that writing narratives is an important skill in History-Social Science. Narratives can be used to tell stories that are important to a culture or to relate past events. Allowing students writing opportunities, such as personal letters or journal entries, helps them practice narrative writing and reinforces learning.

Tell students that when writing narratives, good writers:
- begin the story by telling about the characters and setting.
- introduce a conflict or problem to develop a plot that has a beginning, middle, and end.
- use details and colorful language to draw readers into the story.
- use realistic dialogue to develop characters.
- resolve the conflict or problem by the end of the story.

Narrative writing can be understood by pointing out these elements in well-written works of fiction or in nonfiction works such as biographies, histories, and personal letters. Use Writing Transparency **W**7 to review with students the elements of narrative writing.

IF students have difficulty understanding the importance of using well-chosen details to develop their narratives,

THEN explain to students that the purpose of narrative writing is to provide a context within which the story's plot takes place. To do this, good writers include details that provide insight into why the characters' actions are important or memorable.

Preview Culminating Writing Activity:
Write a Colonial Narrative

In the activity on pp. **96**T27–T28, students will apply the skill of narrative writing. They will write a short work of historical fiction in the form of a letter from a young colonist to a relative or friend back in England.

Writing Support
Unit Skill
Write Narratives
  Lessons 1, 4, 5   ELA 5WA2.1

 • Lesson Assessments,
   pp. **70**T6, **84**T6, **88**T6
Culminating Writing Activity,
pp. **96**T10–T11
 • Writing Transparencies,
   W7, **W**8
 • Writing Models,
   pp. **96**T12–T13
Additional Skills
Write Persuasive Compositions
  Lessons 2, 7   ELA 5WA2.4
Write Research Reports
  Lesson 3   ELA 5WA2.3
Write Responses to Literature
  Lesson 6   ELA 5WA2.2

Have students complete the Study Journal as they go through the unit.

Name:

Study Journal

Unit 4

In this unit you will learn about how European colonists began their settlements in North America, focusing on the English colonies. You will also understand colonial governments and economic systems and the religious and social movements taking place at that time. Complete the activities on these pages as you read the unit.

What I know about . . .

European colonies in North America:

Answers will vary depending on student's knowledge of the subject.

English Colonial Regions

Classify information about the English colonies in the chart below.

Colonial Region	Resources	Early Leaders	Religious Groups	Economic Activities
New England Colonies	Timber, esp. pine Fish, esp. cod, mackerel	William Bradford John Winthrop Thomas Hooker Roger Williams	Puritans Separatists (Pilgrims)	Farming Trade Forestry Fishing
Middle Colonies	Animal furs Fertile soil Timber Iron	Duke of York William Penn	Quakers and many other groups	Trapping Farming Mining Cattle ranching Shipping
Southern Colonies	Fish Timber Fertile soil (rice, indigo, tobacco)	John Smith Lord Baltimore James Oglethorpe	Catholics Anglicans	Plantation cash crops

Complete these sections as you read the unit.

Fill in facts to support the generalization below:

Fact
Thousands joined Baptists, Methodists, or other new religious groups.

The First Great Awakening had many effects on the colonies.

Fact
Religious groups set up new schools and universities.

Fact
Many colonists questioned authority on religion and other issues.

Fact
Many colonists took up a common set of ideas about politics and religion.

List two ways slavery changed life in the Americas. Use two words from the list below in your responses:

- auction
- cash crop
- economy
- indentured servant
- plantation
- proponent
- proprietor
- rebel

1. Answers may vary but should indicate an understanding of the vocabulary words in the historical context of slavery.

2. _____

Fill in the time line below with the correct events.

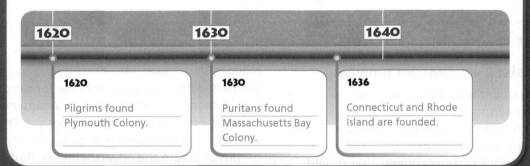

1620	**1630**	**1640**
1620	**1630**	**1636**
Pilgrims found Plymouth Colony.	Puritans found Massachusetts Bay Colony.	Connecticut and Rhode Island are founded.

I have learned . . .

_____

Colonial Newspaper

Students will create a colonial newspaper to illustrate the people, ideas, and events that shaped the development of the English colonies in North America.

1 Editorials

Materials: 8-1/2 x 11 paper, art supplies

Show students some examples of editorials and discuss how editorials are used to express opinions. Brainstorm with students a list of topics from the unit that would make good editorials (Should we be able to worship freely? Do the English colonies really need slavery? etc.). Assign students individually or in small groups to write an editorial that is three paragraphs in length. When editorials are complete, form the class into a large editorial committee. Have students place all the advertisements, cartoons, news stories, and editorials into chronological order and sort them into several newspapers. Then break the class into teams and have them arrange and paste the newspaper materials onto large sheets of chart paper to create their edition of the newspaper. The team should create a masthead and a date for their issue of the newspaper.

2 News Stories

Materials: 8-1/2 x 11 paper, art supplies

Show students some examples of news stories. Brainstorm with students a list of topics from the unit that might make good stories. Assign students individually or in small groups to write a story that is three paragraphs in length. Post the stories in the classroom.

3 Advertisements

Materials: 3 x 5 cards, art supplies

Explain to students that they will create pieces of a colonial newspaper. The whole class will then combine the items created by individual students into a newspaper. Brainstorm with students a list of the kinds of advertisements that should appear in their newspaper. You might consider describing things for sale during colonial times in the stores of the local wigmaker, silversmith, milliner, shoemaker, etc.; describing a carpentry business; offering a farm or horse for sale; seeking employment; advertising to hire a gardener or tutor; or offering to transport goods to England on a ship. Assign students individually or in small groups to create the advertisements. Post the advertisements in the classroom.

4 Political Cartoons

Materials: 8-1/2 x 11 paper, art supplies

Show students some examples of political cartoons. Brainstorm with students a list of topics from the unit that might make good political cartoons (a cartoon that shows that the English colonial system is better than the French or Spanish systems, for example). Assign students individually or in small groups to create the cartoons. Post the cartoons in the classroom.

Newspaper Rubric

4	Student completes one advertisement, one political cartoon, one news story, and/or one editorial. The student's work is accurate and articulate. Student works cooperatively in teams and actively contributes to classroom discussions and activities.
3	Student completes one advertisement, one political cartoon, one news story, and/or one editorial. The student's work is mostly accurate. Student works cooperatively in teams and actively contributes to classroom discussions and activities.
2	Student, with encouragement, completes one advertisement, one political cartoon, one news story and one editorial. The student's work contains some inaccurate information. Student works in teams and contributes to classroom discussions and activities when encouraged.
1	Student does not complete one advertisement, one political cartoon, one news story, and/or one editorial. The student's work is not accurate. Student does not work cooperatively in teams or contribute to classroom discussions and activities.

What influenced where Europeans settled in North America?

🐻 **California Objective H-SS 5.4.1** Understand the influence of location and physical setting on the founding of the original 13 colonies, and identify on a map the locations of the colonies and the American Indian nations already inhabiting these areas.

STANDARDS TRACE	
Introduce	Reinforce
pp. **67** T4, **67–70**	pp. **70** T1–T5, **71–72**

✔ Core Instruction

Content Paths

Text Path, p. 67 T4
Student Text, pp. **67–70**
Skill: Resource Maps

Alternate Instruction

 Digital Path, p. 70 T1
Video: *The Thirteen Colonies*

 Active Path, pp. 70 T2–T4
Colonial Williamsburg
Activity: Character Cards

Big Ideas

Students Will Learn

Resources drew many English settlers to North America in the 1600s.

The Southern Colonies were well suited to agriculture.

Colonists in New England used natural resources.

The Middle Colonies offered important resources also.

Teacher Background

Land ownership was the surest path to wealth in colonial times, and areas rich in resources such as timber and water drew settlers to establish their colonies near Atlantic harbors, rivers, and wooded areas. After the Pilgrims first landed at the northern tip of Cape Cod, they founded Plymouth on the shores of Massachusetts Bay. They chose the site for their colony because of its sheltered harbor and large freshwater brook. The wooded hills promised timber and farming opportunities.

Common Misconception: Students may believe that Plymouth was the first colony and that Columbus came on the Mayflower. Explain that in 1607, Jamestown became the first permanent English colony, and Columbus first arrived in the Americas more than 100 years earlier on the Santa María, with her sister ships, the Niña and the Pinta.

Indigo was a valuable resource in South Carolina. It was used to dye many kinds of cloth. Eliza Lucas Pinckney, the daughter of a plantation owner in South Carolina, managed three plantations after her father was sent away for military duty. She experimented with ginger, cotton, alfalfa, and indigo, and by the 1740s began to market indigo cloth.

Settlers experimented with various resources. Throughout New England, maple trees were used to make sugar. They planted crops such as wheat, corn, and apples and raised livestock such as pigs, cattle, and sheep. Cranberries were harvested from the bogs and swamps of southeastern Massachusetts. In Maine potatoes, oats, hay, and blueberries were farmed. The town of Strawberry Banke, which today is Portsmouth, New Hampshire, used rich forest resources to develop a major shipbuilding industry.

The sandy soil and long growing season in Delaware, New Jersey, and western Long Island allowed for the production of cranberries, watermelons, potatoes, cauliflower, sweet corn, onions, and other crops. New Jersey became known as the Garden State because of its rich agricultural resources. The Pennsylvania Dutch in Lancaster County rotated crops of wheat, clover, corn, potatoes, and tobacco.

Reading Transparency R14

 Make Generalizations Use the transparency before teaching the lesson. After reading the passage, guide students to make the generalization that *people from England came to America for a better life.*

Root Words Recall that root words are the smallest part of a word with meaning. Ask students to identify *plant* as the root word of *plantation*.

Audio Student Text

digital 🔊 A digital audio version of the Student Text is available for students needing auditory support.

Introduce Lesson Vocabulary

For definitions, see p. 67. Read and discuss the terms together. Ask groups of students to create a sentence for each vocabulary word. Have students share their sentences aloud or write them on the board.

plantation	cash crop	proprietor
indentured servant	grant	self-sufficient

digital Lesson Pretest

• Ongoing Assessment pp. **67**T4, **70**T1, **70**T2

• Lesson Assessment p. **70**T6

digital Lesson Quiz

English Learners

Colonies Review concepts related to location.

Beginning (Level 1): Use the map on p. 70 as you discuss the location of the colonies. Help students use the words *above, between,* and *below* as they describe the locations.

Intermediate (Levels 2–3): Use the map on p. 70 as you help students compare the resources in each region. Model the format using *more, less,* or *fewer: The New England Colonies had more fish than the Southern Colonies. The New England Colonies had less wheat than the Middle Colonies.*

Advanced (Levels 4–5): Make a T-chart on the board to list characteristics of New England farms and Southern plantations. Write student responses in the appropriate columns.

digital 🔊 **Audio Student Text**

Extra Support

Make Generalizations Ask students to use generalizations to describe the climate, way of life, and economy in the New England, Southern, and Middle Colonies.

Cause and Effect Help students make a cause-and-effect chart for each of the three colonial regions. For each colonial region, have students describe cause-and-effect relationships between the climate of the region and the way of life of the colonists who lived there.

digital 🔊 **Audio Student Text**

Inclusion/Special Needs

Use a Model Help students make a three-column chart labeled for the New England, Middle, and Southern Colonies. Have students list the resources available in each region.

Evaluate Ask students to think about colonial life in the 1600s. Ask them which region they would like to have lived in and why. Help them base their responses on the information in the lesson.

digital 🔊 **Audio Student Text**

Challenge

Compare and Contrast Ask students to compare the major resources in each region during the 1600s to the region's major resources today. Discuss the extent to which the economy of each region has changed and/or remained the same over the last 400 years.

Predict Ask students what type of trade they think might have existed between the colonies in the three different regions. Ask them to identify the goods and resources each region would have had to offer the others.

LESSON 1
Overview

LESSON 1
Text Path

LESSON 1
Digital Path

LESSON 1
Active Path

LESSON 1
Assessment

LESSON 1 What influenced where Europeans settled in North America? 🐻 H-SS 5.4.1

| **Path Prep** | **Pacing** ⏱ 35 MINUTES | **Materials**
• Student Text, pp. **67–70**
• Student Text Transparencies, pp. **67–70**
• *Find Out More* Handout, p. **70**T5 | **Assessment**
• ⬤ digital Lesson Pretest
• Lesson Assessment, p. **70**T6
• ⬤ digital Lesson Quiz |

1 Build Background

Activate Prior Knowledge Invite students in the class who have relocated from one community to another to give reasons for their move, such as new jobs, better schools, more activities, or to be closer to family. Similarly, people moved from Europe to North America to make better lives for themselves and their families.

Preview the Lesson Read *Set the Scene* with the class. Draw students' attention to the resource map on p. 70. The rich resources of North America motivated Europeans to leave familiar surroundings for the new land. Tell students they will learn that many things influenced where Europeans settled in North America.

Introduce Vocabulary After completing the vocabulary activity on p. 67, remind students that as they read these lessons, breaking a difficult word into recognizable parts often helps find its meaning.

2 Teach

Read Together (pp. **68–69**) Explain to students that the concept of regions is itself a generalization by assuming that all people or land of an area have similar characteristics. Making such generalizations for colonial regions makes it easier to organize and remember new information.

Reading Informational Text As students read this lesson and others in the unit, point out to students that the information is often presented by colonial region.

⬤ digital ◀)) **Audio Student Text**

Summarize When writing their answers to the Lesson Summary on p. 69, encourage students to compare and contrast the environments of the Southern and New England Colonies.

Skill: Resource Maps ⬤ CST 4 (p. **70**) In the North American Colonies, the unique resources of each region influenced how the colonies developed. The same idea holds true today. Review with students what resources have influenced California's development.

Ongoing Assessment ★

▶ **IF** students are having difficulty naming details that support the generalization about colonists seeking a better life (Question 1),

▶ **THEN** encourage them to put the generalization in their own words or into a question, such as *Why did people come to the colonies?* or *What were the benefits of coming to the colonies?*

3 Assess and Extend

Lesson Assessment (p. **70**T6)

Extend Have students use the *Student Atlas* almanac section to research major resources of the original thirteen states today and compare these with the resources of the original colonies.

Find Out More ⬤ CST 5 (p. **70**T5) Have students read the page and discuss why Raleigh might have started a colony on this island. *(southern climate was mild; boats could dock easily; there were fish to eat; they might feel safer)*

Name:

H-SS 5.4.1 Understand the influence of location and physical setting on the founding of the original 13 colonies, and identify on a map the locations of the colonies and the American Indian nations already inhabiting these areas.

Unit 4 • Life in the Colonies

Lesson 1

What influenced where Europeans settled in North America?

SET THE SCENE What would make you and your family leave home and move to a new place? European explorers began arriving in North America in the late 1400s. When other Europeans heard their stories of rich land and large forests, many people decided to move to North America.

Preview the Lesson

Vocabulary

plantation *(n.)* a large farm with many workers who lived on the land they worked

cash crop *(n.)* a crop that is grown to be sold for profit

proprietor *(n.)* an owner

indentured servant *(n.)* a person who agreed to work for an amount of time in exchange for the cost of housing, food, and the voyage to North America

self-sufficient *(adj.)* having the ability to produce most everything that one needs

grant *(v.)* to give something formally to someone

Vocabulary Activity The root word in *proprietor* is related to the root word in *property*. The suffix -*or* means "one who." Circle the suffix in the vocabulary word above. How does knowing these word parts help you understand the meaning of the word?

People

Eliza Lucas Pinckney

⏵ Reading: Make Generalizations

A *generalizations* is a statement that is true most of the time. It is based on facts. As you read the first section on page 68, underline facts that will help you make the generalization that many English settlers came to North America to seek a better life.

67

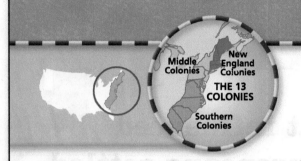

English Settlers Arrive

In the 1600s, English settlers began founding successful colonies along the Atlantic coast of North America. When people in England heard about this land's many resources, more people began moving to the colonies. Many did so to own their own land, to seek gold and silver, and to make money from the fur trade. Over time, different colonial regions developed based on the area's climate and resources.

The Southern Colonies

The warm climate and rich soil of the Southern Colonies were well suited for agriculture. Settlers throughout the colonies established small farms, but settlers in the South realized that their region would also support **plantations,** or large farms with many workers who lived on the land they worked. On plantations, farmers grew cash crops, such as tobacco and rice. **Cash crops** are crops that are grown to be sold for profit. In 1744 Eliza Lucas Pinckney raised the colonies' first successful crop of indigo, a plant that can be made into a blue dye. Indigo soon became another important plantation cash crop.

To work in their fields, **proprietors,** or owners, brought workers from England. Many of these workers were **indentured servants,** or people who agreed to work for an amount of time in exchange for housing, food, and the cost of the voyage to North America.

In the Southern Colonies, cash crops such as tobacco, indigo, and rice were grown on large plantations.

1. ⊙ Make Generalizations **What facts lead to the generalization that people came to the colonies to seek a better life?**

✏ They came to own land, to seek gold and silver, or to make money from the fur trade.

2. **How did the land and climate of the Southern Colonies affect agriculture?** *Cause and Effect*

✏ The Southern Colonies' warm climate and good soil led to the development of small farms and large farms called plantations.

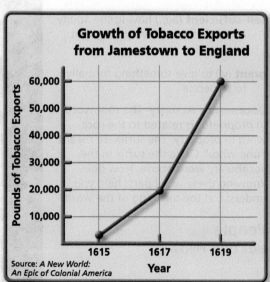

Growth of Tobacco Exports from Jamestown to England

(Line graph: Pounds of Tobacco Exports vs. Year)

Source: *A New World: An Epic of Colonial America*

The New England Colonies

Unlike the Southern Colonies, the cold climate and rocky soil of the New England Colonies could not easily support large plantations. Instead, colonists there used the region's other natural resources to meet their needs. Shipbuilders used tall, white pine trees to build ship masts. Colonists also fished for cod and mackerel.

Many people in New England were self-sufficient farmers. To be **self-sufficient** is to have the ability to produce most everything one needs. Many families lived on small farms. They grew crops, raised livestock, and hunted animals for food. They cut lumber from trees to build homes and make tools.

The Middle Colonies

The Middle Colonies also offered settlers many important resources. The Dutch first settled New Netherlands and profited from the fur trade. England later took over the area and granted some people large areas of land to settle. To **grant** is to give something formally to someone. Some colonists established farms and grew wheat as a cash crop. <u>Because of the many good harbors, the Middle Colonies also became important for shipping.</u> Philadelphia harbor became a seaport and a shipbuilding center. New Amsterdam, later renamed New York City, also became an important seaport.

3. How were farms in New England different from farms in the Southern Colonies?

Compare and Contrast

Farms in Southern Colonies included large plantations, but in New England the region's rocky soil and cold climate led colonists to develop small, self-sufficient, family farms.

Cod and other fish became important resources to the New England colonies.

4. Underline a sentence that tells why shipping became important in the Middle Colonies.

Cause and Effect

Summary Answer The warm climate and rich soil in the South; trees and fish in New England; and good harbors in the Middle.

Summary

Early colonists used their area's resources to live. How did geography and climate affect where people settled in North America?

Unit 4 Lesson 1 • **69**

Skill

Resource Maps

Learn More A resource map shows the resources of an area. The resource map below shows the resources in the New England Colonies, the Middle Colonies, and the Southern Colonies of North America. It also shows the major American Indian groups of the area. In most cases, the resources of an area determined what kinds of economic activities developed there. As you have learned, resources also affected relationships between Europeans and American Indians. Use the map legend below to identify the major crops and goods produced in colonial America. Then answer the questions.

Try It

1. Underline the cash crops in the map legend. *Identify*

2. Circle the name of the colonial region where fish were most plentiful. *Identify*

3. Place a check mark next to an American Indian group that lived in the Middle Colonies. *Identify*

4. In the map legend, circle the resource found in all three colonial regions. *Analyze*

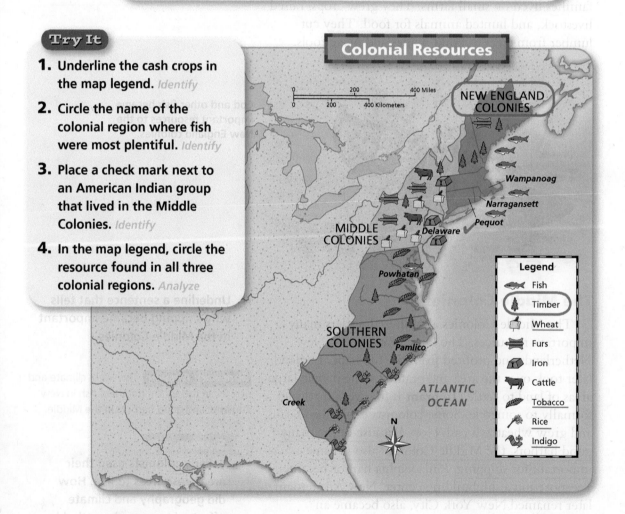

Colonial Resources

NEW ENGLAND COLONIES

Wampanoag

Narragansett

Pequot

MIDDLE COLONIES

Delaware

Powhatan

SOUTHERN COLONIES

Pamlico

Creek

ATLANTIC OCEAN

Legend
- Fish
- Timber
- Wheat
- Furs
- Iron
- Cattle
- Tobacco
- Rice
- Indigo

Alternate Instruction

Digital Path

LESSON 1 **What influenced where Europeans settled in North America?**

🐻 **H-SS 5.4.1**

Path Prep

Pacing
50 MINUTES

Materials
· Video: *The Thirteen Colonies*
· Interactive Practice: *Settling in North America*
· Print Partner: *Resources Affect Settlement*
· **digital** 🔊 Audio Student Text

Assessment
· **digital** Lesson Pretest
· Lesson Assessment, p. **70**T6
· **digital** Lesson Quiz

1 Build Background

Activate Prior Knowledge Ask: *Why do families move from one community to another?* Then have students speculate about what North America had to offer European settlers.

Introduce Vocabulary Introduce the lesson vocabulary words using the print or digital cards.

Lesson Introduction Launch the Lesson Introduction, which asks the question, "What influenced where Europeans settled in North America?"

2 Teach

Video As students view *The Thirteen Colonies,* have them consider these questions:
• What natural resources did each of the three colonial regions have to offer?
• In what ways did these resources affect the settlement of the colonial regions?

Interactive Practice Launch the activity, *Settling in North America.* The activity will help students understand that the settlement and growth of the New England, Middle, and Southern Colonies was, in large part, determined by the resources available in each region.

Print Partner Ask students to complete the Print Partner. In the activity, students

will describe through writing or pictures the resources, crops, and goods associated with each of the three colonial regions.

digital 🔊 **Audio Student Text**

Ongoing Assessment ★

▶ **IF** students are struggling to understand why natural resources influenced the settlement of the colonies,

▶ **THEN** write "Wood," "Wildlife," and "Soil" on the board. Ask students to name products related to each natural resource. Record their ideas. When several items are listed for each resource, guide students to recognize that settlers were able to build, hunt, and grow many different things as a result of the colonies' natural resources.

3 Assess and Extend

digital **Lesson Quiz** Have students check their understanding of the lesson by answering the questions. Review the correct answers with students after they complete the page.

Lesson Assessment Use the assessment on p. **70**T6 to evaluate students' understanding of the lesson.

Extend Ask each student to choose one of the thirteen colonies to research. Have them compare and contrast how the Europeans and the local American Indian groups living in the colony used the natural resources of the area. Students can report their findings in a chart.

Alternate Instruction

Active Path

Colonial Williamsburg

LESSON 1 What influenced where Europeans settled in North America?

H-SS 5.4.1

Description: Students will use character cards and a map to explore the factors that led colonists to settle the colonies and identify what American Indian groups were already living there.

Path Prep

Pacing	Materials	Assessment
50 MINUTES	· *Big Book Atlas* or *Student Atlas* · Colored pencils, scissors, glue or tape · Handouts, pp. **70**T3–T4 · Student Text, p. **70**	· **digital** Lesson Pretest · Lesson Assessment, p. **70**T6 · **digital** Lesson Quiz

1 Build Background

Activate Prior Knowledge Give students the *Map of the Thirteen Colonies* handout, p. **70**T3. Identify the individual colonies and the three regions. Use the map from the Student Text on p. 70 to discuss the characteristics of the regions, including climate, natural resources, and geography. Stress how each region is unique.

Introduce Vocabulary Go over the vocabulary words *plantation, cash crop, proprietor, indentured servant, self-sufficient,* and *grant.*

2 Teach

Introduce Activity Explain that students will use character cards to explore some of the reasons colonists settled in particular regions of the English colonies.

Activity Steps

1. Divide the class into groups. Give each group the *Character Cards* handout, p. **70**T4. Have them cut apart the cards and turn the stack of cards face down.

2. Have students take turns turning over a card, reading it aloud, and discussing which region is most appropriate for that colonist. Have students complete each card by indicating the region and writing the reason for selecting that region on the back of the card.

3. Review the *Map of the Thirteen Colonies* handout, p. **70**T3, to see the locations of American Indian groups in the colonies. For each character card, have students list the American Indian groups with which the colonist may have interacted.

Ongoing *Assessment* ★

▶ **IF** students have difficulty connecting natural resources and geographic factors to colonists' reasons for settling each region,

▶ **THEN** have them make a chart that shows what resources are available for each region shown on the map.

3 Assess and Extend

Assess On the board, make three columns labeled *New England, Middle,* and *Southern.* One character card at a time, have a member of each group tape that card in the column for the region the group selected, and share the reasons for the group's decision.
Answer Key–1) Southern; 2) Middle; 3) New England; 4) Middle or Southern; 5) New England; 6) New England or Middle; 7) Southern; 8) Middle; and 9) New England.

Lesson Assessment (p. **70**T6)

Extend Assign each group one of the regions and have them create a presentation explaining why a new American colonist should settle there.

LESSON 1 Overview

LESSON 1 Text Path

LESSON 1 Digital Path

LESSON 1 Active Path

LESSON 1 Assessment

Name: _____

Unit 4 Lesson 1

Map of the Thirteen Colonies

Directions: Label each of the thirteen colonies.

Connecticut	New Hampshire	Pennsylvania
Delaware	New Jersey	Rhode Island
Georgia	New York	South Carolina
Maryland	North Carolina	Virginia
Massachusetts		

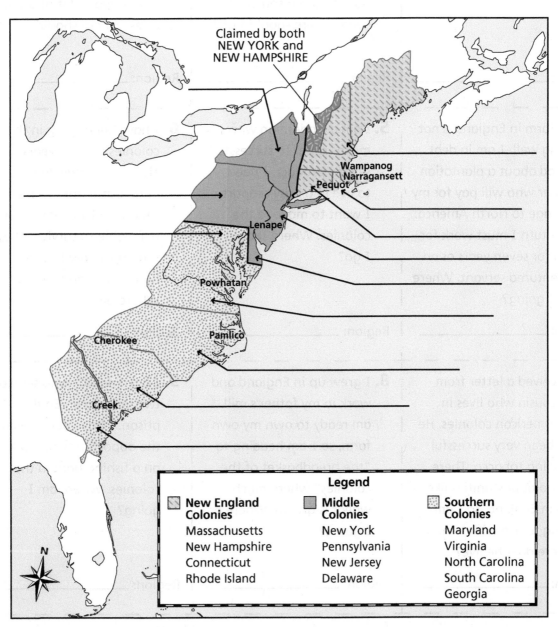

Colonial Williamsburg

Unit 4 Lesson 1

Character Cards

Directions: Cut apart the cards and stack them face down. Take turns drawing a card, reading it aloud, and discussing which region of the colonies is most appropriate for the colonist to live in.

1. There is very little land available in England. I have enough money to allow me to own a large plantation. Where should I go?

Region: _____

2. I am a blacksmith's apprentice who is ready to have my own shop. I want to move to the colonies and maybe get into iron mining. If I want to live close to the resources I need, where should I go?

Region: _____

3. Most of the trees in England have been cut down. So I have been sent to the colonies to purchase as much lumber as possible. I need a seaport that is near a lot of usable trees. Where should I go?

Region: _____

4. My farm in England is not doing well. I am in debt. I read about a plantation owner who will pay for my passage to North America. In return I must work for him for seven years as an indentured servant. Where am I going?

Region: _____

5. I am a tradesman who makes rope. To successfully sell my product, I need to live in a busy seaport. I want to move to the colonies. Where should I go?

Region: _____

6. I have been living in the colonies for two years. The winters have been hard, but thanks to the American Indians we have been able to survive. They taught us how to fish, hunt, and trap animals. Where am I?

Region: _____

7. I received a letter from my cousin who lives in the American colonies. He has been very successful growing tobacco. There are no opportunities like this in England, so I am going to live with him. Where does he live?

Region: _____

8. I grew up in England and work in my father's mill. I am ready to own my own farm, so I am heading to "the breadbasket of the colonies" where much wheat is grown. Where am I going?

Region: _____

9. I am a debtor who served two years in an English prison. I have been given the opportunity to work on a fishing boat in the colonies. Where am I going?

Region: _____

Unit 4 Lesson 1

Early Colonies: Roanoke

England's earliest attempts at starting colonies were not always successful. Settlers at Roanoke faced problems related to the colony's location. Here is a description of the early days of the colony. As you read, think about what role location played in the success of the settlements.

Roanoke

In the late 1500s, England began trying to establish colonies in North America. A close advisor to Queen Elizabeth, Walter Raleigh (RAH lee), offered to organize the first colony. Raleigh was a soldier who explored North America in the early 1580s. He knew of a place called Roanoke Island off the coast of what is now North Carolina.

The first group of colonists Raleigh sent to Roanoke Island landed in 1585. They faced a difficult winter during which they had trouble finding food. In 1586 the starving English settlers returned home.

But Raleigh was not ready to give up the idea of starting a colony in North America. In 1587 John White led more than 100 men, women, and children to Roanoke Island. Almost one month later, a baby girl was born in the colony. She was named Virginia Dare and was the first English person born in the Americas. This colony also struggled. When supplies ran out, White sailed back to England. However, he found his country at war with Spain. England could not spare any ships to send supplies to the colony.

White was not able to return to Roanoke Island until August 1590. When he arrived, everyone had disappeared. The only clue White found was the word *CROATOAN* carved into a tree. "Croatoan" was the name of an American Indian group that lived near Roanoke Island.

No one knows what happened to the Roanoke settlement. Some historians think the colonists may have been captured by Spanish soldiers. They may have died in battles with American Indians. Another possibility is that the starving colonists moved south to live with the Croatoan people. Because the mystery remains unsolved, the Roanoke Island settlement is known as "The Lost Colony."

Name: _____

What influenced where Europeans settled in North America?

1. 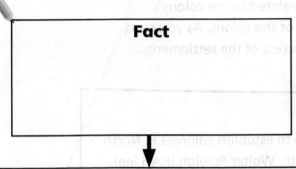 **Make Generalizations:** Fill in the chart below with two facts that support the generalization.

Fact	Fact

↓ ↓

Generalization
Many New England colonists used the region's natural resources.

2. *Understand* How did **proprietors** use **indentured servants** in the Southern Colonies?

_____

_____

3. *Analyze* Explain the effects of resources and location on the development of the Middle Colonies.

_____

_____

4. *Synthesize* The resources available in some colonies helped the colonists survive. If you were moving to a new place, what types of resources would you need to survive? Explain your answer.

_____

_____

5. **Write a Journal Entry** You are an early colonist living in one of the colonial regions. Write a journal entry describing the physical setting of your colony, the resources that were available, and who else lived there.

Link to Science Suppose you were living in the Southern Colonies and wanted to grow a **cash crop** on a **plantation**. Research the type of climate you would need in order to successfully grow your crop.

© Pearson Scott Foresman

Lesson 1 Assessment

Answers

1.

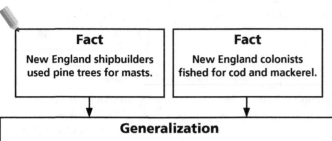

Fact	Fact
New England shipbuilders used pine trees for masts.	New England colonists fished for cod and mackerel.

Generalization

Many New England colonists used the region's natural resources.

2. Indentured servants worked in exchange for housing, food, and the cost of their trip from England to North America.

3. Both resources and location made the Middle Colonies appealing to settlers. Resources could be traded. The location made shipping possible.

4. Students should be able to justify why they would need the resources they mention.

5. Journal entries should provide accurate and detailed descriptions of the physical setting of the colony, its available resources, and the people living there. Use the following narrative writing rubric to score students' journal entries:

4	Student writes a multiple-paragraph narrative that includes accurate and detailed descriptions. Spelling and grammar are correct.
3	Student writes one or two paragraphs that include good descriptive details. Spelling and grammar have a few errors.
2	Student writes a one-paragraph narrative that includes some descriptive details. Spelling and grammar have some serious errors.
1	Narrative is not organized as a paragraph. It has few or no relevant details. There are many serious errors.

Link to ⚬⚬ Science Students' research on climate should support their choice of cash crop.

Intervention

Reading Skill Mini-Lesson   `ELA 5RC2.4`

Go back into the text and reread "The New England Colonies." Ask students to look for facts that will support the generalization: "Many New England colonists used the region's natural resources." Review that they used trees to build masts and they fished for food. Have students explain how these facts support the generalization.

Analysis Skill Mini-Lesson   `CST 5`

To help students understand how relative advantages and disadvantages of location can change over time, point out that Philadelphia and New York City are still major seaports. Discuss whether shipping is still as important as it was in colonial days.

Writing Skill Mini-Lesson   `ELA 5WA2.1`

Tell students that a good narrative about a place includes descriptive sensory details.

Have students suggest a colonial region and brainstorm with them what they would expect to see there. Students should suggest details that could help the reader picture what that region would look like, adding details to complete the journal entry.

Science Support   `S4.b`

Help students choose a crop and use encyclopedias or *.gov, .org,* or *.edu* Web sites to find climate information for the crop.

Who founded the colonies and why?

 California Objective H-SS 5.4.2 Identify the major individuals and groups responsible for the founding of the various colonies and the reasons for their founding (e.g., John Smith, Virginia; Roger Williams, Rhode Island; William Penn, Pennsylvania; Lord Baltimore, Maryland; William Bradford, Plymouth; John Winthrop, Massachusetts).

STANDARDS TRACE	
Introduce	Reinforce
pp. **71** T4, **71–76**	pp. **76** T1–T5 **77–80**

Content Paths	✓ **Core Instruction**	**Alternate Instruction**	
	△ **Text Path,** p. **71** T4 Student Text, pp. **71–74** Skill: Classifying and Sorting	**Digital Path,** p. **76** T1 Video: *Founding the Colonies*	✋ **Active Path,** pp. **76** T2–T4 *Colonial Williamsburg* Activity: Research Colonial Leaders

Big Ideas

Teacher Background

Students Will Learn

The English established colonies in North America.

The colony of Carolina began from a grant from King Charles II in 1663. Carolina settlers were unhappy with the proprietary government, which was based in Charles Towne (later Charleston). North Carolina and South Carolina became separate provinces but were still subject to proprietary rule until 1729, when royal rule began. Population increased, and settlement expanded in North Carolina, but hostility toward British rule remained until 1775.

Many Southern Colonies were founded as corporate and proprietary colonies.

John White was an artist and cartographer who made three westward sea voyages toward the Americas. The sketchings and paintings he created in Roanoke were used as illustrations in *A Briefe and True Report of the New Found Land of Virginia* by Thomas Hariot. His second trip to Roanoke, shortly before the English war with Spain, was unsuccessful because he could not secure a relief expedition for the abandoned settlement.

Common Misconception: Students may not fully understand that proprietor here refers only to those individuals who were awarded licenses from the king of England to supervise and develop land. (It is similar to the arrangements of colonies financed and settled by joint stock companies.) Point out that generally, however, proprietors are just owners of businesses, such as shops, factories, or service providers.

Many New England colonies were founded by Separatists.

William Bradford dedicated his life to the Separatist Church at age twelve, during the Protestant Reformation. He was part of the group of Pilgrims who fled to Holland, where he helped plan the trip to North America on the Mayflower. He was a framer of the Mayflower Compact and was reelected as governor of Plymouth thirty times. The democratic practices Bradford established included town meetings, which are still used in the United States today. Bradford made efforts to unite all Separatist groups in the colonies.

The Middle Colonies were founded by Dutch, Swedish, and English settlers.

As a young English man, William Penn became a Quaker and political liberal. He was jailed for his beliefs several times. After Penn's wealthy father died, Penn used the land King Charles II granted him to establish the colony of Pennsylvania, or "Penn's woods." He made peace with local American Indians and signed a peace treaty with the Lenni Lenape in 1683. He also signed the Charter of Privileges, which allowed for a more democratic government in Pennsylvania. Penn also founded Delaware, which became an important agricultural and trading colony.

Reading Transparency R15

Compare and Contrast Use the transparency before teaching the lesson to identify signal words for comparisons and contrasts. Underline the following words: *like, however,* and *unlike.*

Root Words Have students recall root words as "the form of the word when the prefixes and suffixes (affixes) have been removed." Guide students to identify *pure* and *separate* as the root words for *Puritan* and *Separatists.*

Audio Student Text

digital ◀)) A digital audio version of the Student Text is available for students needing auditory support.

Introduce Lesson Vocabulary

For definitions, see p. 71. Look at the words and definitions together. Have students work in pairs with their vocabulary cards and take turns reading aloud a definition to match with the correct term.

persecution   Separatists   pilgrim

Puritan   dissenter

Assessment

digital Lesson Pretest

• Ongoing Assessment pp. **71**T4, **76**T1, **76**T2

• Lesson Assessment p. **76**T6

digital Lesson Quiz

Universal Access

English Learners

Charts Use a chart to ask and answer questions.

Beginning (Level 1): Write the dates from the chart on p. 76 on individual index cards. Hold up each card and ask students: *What colony was founded in (1634)?* Point to the chart as you reply: *Maryland.* Have students continue this format with a partner.

Intermediate (Levels 2–3): Use the chart on p. 76 to model questions for students using *before* and *after: New York was founded before Georgia. Delaware was founded after Virginia.* Have students refer to the chart as they make their own sentences.

Advanced (Levels 4–5): Have students read the reasons on p. 76 that the Thirteen Colonies were founded. On a separate piece of paper, have students group colonies with similar reasons together. Have students write sentences to compare and contrast the number of reasons in each group.

digital ◀)) Audio Student Text

Extra Support

Take Notes Help students make a three-column chart. In the first column, describe the three general locations of the colonies. In the second column, write who came to live in the colony, and in the third column, tell why people came to that colony.

Identify Main Idea Have students use each vocabulary word in sentences identifying the main idea and supporting details about each of the three colonial regions.

digital ◀)) Audio Student Text

Inclusion/Special Needs

Identify Key Words Help students make a map showing the general location and extent of the New England, Southern, and Middle Colonies. Help students label the map with key words and names from the lesson which are associated with each region.

Use Maps Look at a map of the northeastern United States with students. Help them find the location of the colonies and cities mentioned in the lesson. Discuss the scale of the map and the actual distances separating what used to be the colonies.

digital ◀)) Audio Student Text

Challenge

Analyze Reread this statement from the lesson to students: "Although many early colonists came to Massachusetts hoping to escape religious persecution, religion within the colony was strict." Discuss the contradictory nature of this statement and whether or not there truly was religious freedom in the colonies.

Compare and Contrast Ask students to write a brief paper comparing and contrasting the settlements in the New England, Southern, and Middle Colonies. Tell them to compare how the settlements were colonized, the leadership, the religion, and where the colonists came from and why.

LESSON 2
Digital Path

LESSON 2
Active Path

LESSON 2
Assessment

LESSON 2 Who founded the colonies and why?

🐻 H-SS 5.4.2

Path Prep

Pacing	Materials	Assessment
⏱ 50 MINUTES	• Student Text, pp. **71–76** • Student Text Transparencies, pp. **71–76** • *Find Out More* Handout, p. **76**T5 • Classroom calendar or chart	• (digital) Lesson Pretest • Lesson Assessment, p. **76**T6 • (digital) Lesson Quiz

1 Build Background

Activate Prior Knowledge On the board, write the words *school, friends, family,* and *freedom.* Ask students to choose one category and think about what their lives would be like without it. For example, what if students felt unwelcome at school, or they were not free to make their own choices? Would they want to move to a new place? Many Europeans traveled to the colonies looking for a better life.

Preview the Lesson Read *Set the Scene* with the class and discuss the picture on p. 71. Point out that people who left Europe for North America were taking a big risk. Tell students they will read that many Europeans took great risks for a number of reasons.

Introduce Vocabulary After students complete the vocabulary activity on p. 71, help them clarify the differences among *Separatists, pilgrims,* and *Puritans.*

2 Teach

Read Together (pp. 72–75) After each section, pause to allow students time to scan the text for signal words, such as *like* or *similar*. Remind them to look for ideas in the lesson that are supported by sentences in the text.

Find Out More (p. **76**T5) As students read the lesson, allow time to fill in the new information on the chart. Emphasize how making charts such as this one helps organize large amounts of information.

Reading Informational Text As students read, have them use the locator maps to establish the location of the colonies. When finished reading, review the time line to understand chronology.

(digital) ◀)) **Audio Student Text**

Summarize When writing their answers to the Lesson Summary on p. 75, students should be

encouraged to look for generalizations as well as the facts that support them.

Skill: Classifying and Sorting [CST 1]
(p. 76) Show students a calendar or a chart posted on the classroom wall. Ask students to suppose the information on a calendar were in lines of text such as "Saturday, November 13, School Recital; Sunday, November 14 . . ." Ask why calendars are easier to use in chart form. Then use the Student Text Transparency to help students answer the questions about the chart.

Ongoing *Assessment* ★

▶ **IF** students are struggling to see the compare-and-contrast relationships among the colonists' reasons for settlement (Question 2),

▶ **THEN** encourage them to create Venn diagrams to organize the information.

3 Assess and Extend

Lesson Assessment (p. **76**T6)

Extend Model how to enter information from

the skill lesson on p. 76 into a spreadsheet. With a computer, use the date-sort feature to demonstrate how information can be sorted.

Name:

🐻 **H-SS 5.4.2** Identify the major individuals and groups responsible for the founding of the various colonies and the reasons for their founding (e.g., John Smith, Virginia; Roger Williams, Rhode Island; William Penn, Pennsylvania; Lord Baltimore, Maryland; William Bradford, Plymouth; John Winthrop, Massachusetts).

Unit 4 • Life in the Colonies
Lesson 2

Who founded the colonies and why?

SET THE SCENE Why do people move to new areas? As you have learned, the resources and opportunities in North America attracted many settlers from Europe. But people moved to North America for other reasons too. What other reasons might Europeans have had for founding new colonies?

Preview the Lesson
Vocabulary

persecution *(n.)* unjust treatment

Separatists *(n.)* a group of people from England who wanted to separate themselves from the Church of England

pilgrim *(n.)* a person who travels to a place for religious reasons

Puritan *(n.)* a person from England who wanted to improve the Church of England

dissenter *(n.)* a person whose views are different from those of his or her leaders

Vocabulary Activity Circle the word above that has *pure* as its root word. Underline the word that has *separate* as its root word.

People

John Smith	Thomas Hooker
Lord Baltimore	Roger Williams
James Oglethorpe	Duke of York
William Bradford	William Penn
John Winthrop	

Reading: Compare and Contrast

When you *compare* two or more things, you look for their similarities. When you *contrast* them, you look for their differences. Writers use signal words such as *like* and *similar* to compare things. They use signal words such as *unlike* and *different* to contrast them. As you read the lesson, circle the compare and contrast signal words. ▷

71

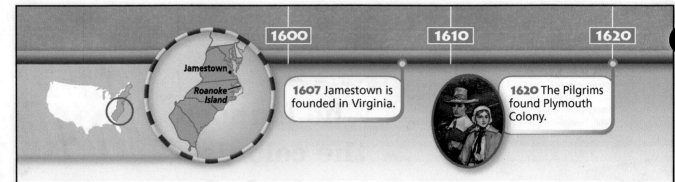

1600 **1610** **1620**

Jamestown

Roanoke Island

1607 Jamestown is founded in Virginia.

1620 The Pilgrims found Plymouth Colony.

The English Establish Colonies

European countries and settlers had many reasons for building colonies. Countries wanted to gain wealth through land and natural resources. Like their home countries, some settlers also hoped to grow rich by owning their own land. In addition, some settlers came to the colonies to escape persecution for their religious beliefs. **Persecution** is unjust treatment. Others wanted the chance to start a new life.

In the late 1500s, English monarchs, or rulers, began giving people charters to form different kinds of colonies in North America. In corporate colonies, the monarch gave control of the land and its settlers to a business. In proprietary colonies, control was given to a proprietor or group of proprietors. In royal colonies, the monarch kept control, usually through appointed officials. By 1752 monarchs had changed many corporate and proprietary colonies into royal colonies.

English businesses sought to profit by founding corporate colonies such as Jamestown.

1. **How were corporate colonies different from royal colonies?**
Compare and Contrast

Corporate colonies were controlled by businesses, but royal colonies were controlled by the English monarch.

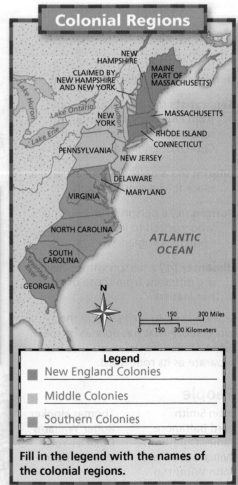

Colonial Regions

NEW HAMPSHIRE

CLAIMED BY NEW HAMPSHIRE AND NEW YORK

MAINE (PART OF MASSACHUSETTS)

Lake Huron

Lake Ontario

Lake Erie

Hudson R.

NEW YORK

MASSACHUSETTS

RHODE ISLAND
CONNECTICUT

PENNSYLVANIA

NEW JERSEY

DELAWARE

VIRGINIA

MARYLAND

NORTH CAROLINA

ATLANTIC OCEAN

SOUTH CAROLINA

Savannah River

GEORGIA

N

0   150   300 Miles
0   150   300 Kilometers

Legend

New England Colonies

Middle Colonies

Southern Colonies

Fill in the legend with the names of the colonial regions.

72 • Life in the Colonies

1630 | **1640** | **1650**

1630
Puritans found Massachusetts Bay Colony.

1636 Thomas Hooker founds Connecticut. Roger Williams founds Rhode Island.

1634 Lord Baltimore founds Maryland.

Founding the Southern Colonies

Many Southern Colonies were started as corporate colonies. John White founded a colony on Roanoke Island as a trading center in 1587. After starting the colony, White returned to England for supplies. When he returned to Roanoke in 1590, all the colonists had disappeared. No one knew what had happened to them.

In 1607 the Virginia Company founded the Jamestown Colony. Illness, poor food, and lack of discipline caused many hardships for the colonists. Less than half of the original colonists survived their first year at Jamestown. Then a new leader named John Smith created a strict rule that food should be given only to people who worked. Working together, the colonists built houses and learned to use the area's resources. After the colonists planted their first successful tobacco crop in 1612, the colony began to thrive.

Other Southern Colonies were founded as proprietary colonies. Lord Baltimore founded Maryland in 1634 as a place for Catholics, who were persecuted in England. Like colonists in Virginia, some colonists in Maryland built large tobacco plantations.

The colony of Carolina was founded by a group of proprietors in 1663. Over time, the region's rich soil and good harbors attracted many settlers. In 1712 the colony divided into North Carolina and South Carolina. These became official royal colonies in 1729.

James Oglethorpe founded Georgia in 1733 for a different reason. He wanted to give English debtors, or people who owed money, a new start as farmers. Few debtors came, but skilled workers and others settled in Georgia.

2. How was Maryland different from other Southern Colonies? How was it similar? *Compare and Contrast*

Different: Many Southern Colonies were started for business reasons; but Maryland was founded for religious purposes. Alike: Maryland and other Southern Colonies had large tobacco plantations.

The development of tobacco crops attracted many colonists and was key to the success of Virginia and other Southern Colonies.

Unit 4 Lesson 2 • **73**

LESSON 2 Overview

LESSON 2 Text Path

LESSON 2 Digital Path

LESSON 2 Active Path

LESSON 2 Assessment

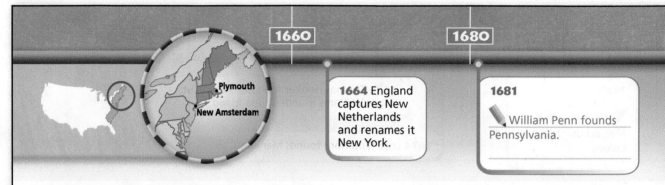

1660   **1680**

Plymouth

New Amsterdam

1664 England captures New Netherlands and renames it New York.

1681

William Penn founds Pennsylvania.

Founding New England Colonies

Unlike most Southern colonists, many colonists came to New England to escape religious persecution. The first of these colonists were **Separatists,** or people who wanted to separate themselves from the Church of England. In 1620 a group of Separatists landed in the area that is now Massachusetts. They founded Plymouth Colony and elected William Bradford as their governor. This first group of New England colonists came to be known as Pilgrims. A **pilgrim** is a person who travels to a place for religious reasons.

In 1630 another group came to New England in search of religious freedom. This group, known as the Puritans, was led by John Winthrop. A **Puritan** was a person from England who wanted to improve the Church of England. Winthrop hoped to start a colony where Puritans could worship as they wanted and be an example to others. He said, "We shall be a City upon a hill, the eyes of all people are on us." The Puritan colony was called the Massachusetts Bay Colony. Its main settlement was the city of Boston.

Although many early colonists came to Massachusetts hoping to escape religious persecution, religion within the colony was strictly controlled. Because of this, people left Massachusetts to start their own colonies. In 1636 Thomas Hooker founded Hartford. Later, the area would become the colony of Connecticut. Roger Williams was known as a **dissenter,** or person whose views are different from those of his or her leaders. He was forced to leave Massachusetts and founded the settlement of Providence in 1636. Later, this area would become the colony of Rhode Island.

3. Make Generalizations **What facts help you make the generalization that most of the New England colonies were founded for religious reasons?**

Possible answers: Pilgrims founded Plymouth; Puritans founded the Massachusetts Bay Colony; and religious dissenters founded Rhode Island.

Some Separatists first sought religious freedom in the Netherlands. In 1620 a group of Separatists sailed from England to North America on the *Mayflower*.

| 1700 | 1720 | 1740 | 1760 |

1729 North and South Carolina become royal colonies.

1733 James Oglethorpe founds Georgia colony.

Founding the Middle Colonies

The founding of the Middle Colonies was different than that of New England and the Southern Colonies. The area was first claimed by the Netherlands and Sweden. In 1624 the Dutch named their colony New Netherlands. They built a trading post called New Amsterdam that became a center for the fur trade.

The area did not stay under Dutch control, however. England already had colonies to the north and south of New Netherlands. King Charles II of England wanted to combine these colonies and to control New Netherlands' rich resources. In 1664 England captured the Dutch colony. The king gave a large part of the colony to his brother James, the Duke of York. The Duke renamed the colony New York, and New Amsterdam became New York City. The Duke then gave part of the land to his friends, who renamed it New Jersey. To pay off a debt, the king also gave William Penn land along the Delaware River. Penn belonged to a religious group called the Quakers. In 1681 he founded the colony of Pennsylvania as a "holy experiment," where people of all religions could live together.

5. In the text, underline the reason why England took over New Netherlands. *Main Idea and Details*

Summary Answer Possible answers: For business reasons, for religious reasons, and for debtors to start a new life

New York City became a valuable colonial trade center because of its important location and good harbor.

Summary

People from England began founding North American colonies in the 1500s. What reasons did people have for founding these colonies?

Unit 4 Lesson 2 • **75**

LESSON 2 Overview

LESSON 2 Text Path

LESSON 2 Digital Path

LESSON 2 Active Path

LESSON 2 Assessment

Skill

Classifying and Sorting

Learn More When you classify information, you sort it into categories. Classifying information makes it easier to compare and contrast it. The chart below classifies information about the thirteen English colonies. In this chart, the colonies are classified and sorted alphabetically by name. The headings at the top of each column can be used to classify the information by other categories. Study the chart, then answer the questions below.

Try It

1. How many colonies are classified alphabetically by the letter *N*? *Identify*

   4

2. Which category would you use to create a time line of when the colonies were founded? *Analyze*

   Year

3. If you classified the colonies according to the year they were founded, which colony would be listed first? Draw a star next to it. *Interpret*

4. Circle the colonies that could be classified as being founded for religious reasons. *Analyze*

Colony	Year	Early Leaders	Reasons for Founding
Connecticut	1639[2]	Thomas Hooker	Farming, trade, political freedom
Delaware	1704[2]	William Penn	Trade, farming
Georgia	1733[1]	James Oglethorpe	Refuge for debtors, colony between Carolinas & Florida
(Maryland)	1634[1]	Lord Baltimore	Refuge for Catholics in North America
(Massachusetts)	1620[1]	William Bradford, John Winthrop	Escape religious persecution in England
New Hampshire	1729[2]	John Wheelwright	Trade, fishing
New Jersey	1664[2]	John Berkeley, George Carteret	Build colony on land captured from Dutch
New York	1664[2]	Duke of York	Build colony on land captured from Dutch
North Carolina	1653[1]	William Berkeley	Farming
(Pennsylvania)	1682[1]	William Penn	Establish Quaker colony in North America
(Rhode Island)	1636[1]	Roger Williams	Establish colony for people of all religions
South Carolina	1670[1]	Anthony Ashley-Cooper	Farming
★ Virginia	1607[1]	John Smith	Establish English colony in North America, search for gold

[1] Settled   [2] Charter granted

Digital Path

LESSON 2 Who founded the colonies and why?

 **H-SS 5.4.2**

| Path Prep | Pacing ⏱ 50 MINUTES | **Materials** · Video: *Founding the Colonies* · Interactive Practice: *Who Founded the Colonies?* · Print Partner: *The Birth of Colonial America* · **digital** 🔊 Audio Student Text | **Assessment** · **digital** Lesson Pretest · Lesson Assessment, p. **76**T6 · **digital** Lesson Quiz |

1 Build Background

Activate Prior Knowledge Tell students that throughout history people have moved away from the countries where they were born. Discuss why people might risk leaving their families and all they know to move to another country.

Introduce Vocabulary Introduce the lesson vocabulary words using the print or digital cards.

Lesson Introduction Launch the Lesson Introduction, which asks the question, "Who founded the colonies and why?"

2 Teach

Video As students view *Founding the Colonies,* have them consider these questions:
• Why did people leave Europe to settle in North America?
• Where were the first settlements located?
• Why were they founded?

Interactive Practice Launch the activity, *Who Founded the Colonies?* The activity will help students understand why different colonies were established in North America and the people responsible for their founding.

Print Partner In this activity, students will write about the founding of the colonies.

digital 🔊 **Audio Student Text**

Ongoing Assessment ★

▶ **IF** students are struggling to identify the leaders of the different colonies,

▶ **THEN** have students make flashcards for the colony leaders presented in the lesson. On each flashcard have students identify the founding leader, the colony, and the year it was founded. Allow time for students to form small groups and quiz one another using the flashcards.

3 Assess and Extend

digital **Lesson Quiz** Have students check their understanding of the lesson content by answering the questions. Review the correct responses with the class.

Lesson Assessment Use the assessment on p. **76**T6 to evaluate students' lesson comprehension.

Extend Assign small groups of students to research one of the colonies discussed in the lesson. Invite each group to learn more about their colony's settlement and early years. Have each group create a poster to share their findings with the class. Tell students to include both pictures and text in their posters. Set aside time for each group to present their work in class.

LESSON 2 Overview

LESSON 2 Text Path

LESSON 2 Digital Path

LESSON 2 Active Path

LESSON 2 Assessment

Active Path

Colonial Williamsburg

LESSON 2 **Who founded the colonies and why?**

🐻 **H-SS 5.4.2**

Description: Students will research a specific colonist to learn about his contributions to the founding of a particular colony.

Path Prep	Pacing	Materials	Assessment
	TWO 50-MINUTE SESSIONS	· Classroom research materials · Chart paper · Handouts, pp. **76**T3–T4	· `digital` Lesson Pretest · Lesson Assessment, p. **76**T6 · `digital` Lesson Quiz

1 Build Background

Activate Prior Knowledge Ask students to describe the characteristics they think the founder of a colony should have. Lead students to consider qualities such as leadership, knowledge, education, occupation, and family background. Record student responses on chart paper and save for the end of the lesson.

Introduce Vocabulary Go over the vocabulary words *persecution, Separatist, pilgrim, Puritan,* and *dissenter.* Ask students which of these words they have heard before and in what context.

2 Teach

Introduce Activity Explain to students that they will research several colonial leaders to determine their reasons for and role in founding an American colony.

Activity Steps

1. Write one founder's name on each of eight sheets of chart paper and place them around the room. Divide the class into eight small groups and assign each group one of the founders. (Note: To examine more than eight founders, consider including the Duke of York, John Wheelwright, John Berkeley, George Carteret, William Berkeley, or Anthony Ashley-Cooper.)

2. Give each group the *Colonial Founders Fact Sheet* handout to use as a research guide. Have students transfer their research

information from the graphic organizer to the appropriate sheet of chart paper.

3. Pass out *The Thirteen Colonies* handout. Conduct a discussion in which students identify the characteristics of the founder they researched, his contributions, and his reasons for founding a colony. As each group presents, students should complete the appropriate section of their graphic organizer for each founder, as well as the information on the map handout.

Ongoing *Assessment* ★

▶ **IF** students have difficulty understanding the concept of a proprietary colony,

▶ **THEN** ask them if the founder they researched owned the colony's land.

3 Assess and Extend

Assess Have students write a paragraph in which they compare and contrast two of the founders.

Lesson Assessment (p. **76**T6)

Extend Have students research Sir Walter Raleigh and John White, who both attempted to start a colony at Roanoke.

Unit 4 Lesson 2

Colonial Founders Fact Sheet

Directions: Fill in the chart with important information, such as the person's contributions to the colony and when the colony was founded.

Person	Important Information
Thomas Hooker	
James Oglethorpe	
John Smith	
Roger Williams	
William Penn	
Lord Baltimore	
William Bradford	
John Winthrop	

Name: _____

The Thirteen Colonies

Directions: Identify early leader(s) of each colony by putting the correct name on each empty line.

Roger Williams	William Penn
Lord Baltimore	John Winthrop
William Bradford	John Smith
James Oglethorpe	Thomas Hooker

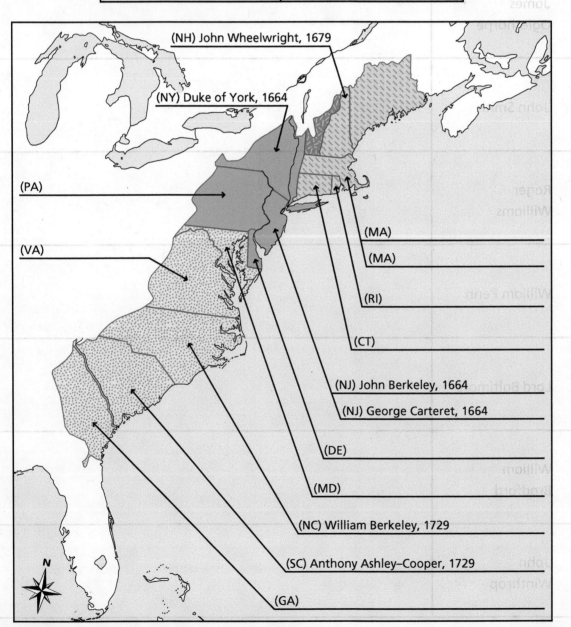

(NH) John Wheelwright, 1679

(NY) Duke of York, 1664

(PA)

(VA)

(MA) _____

(MA) _____

(RI) _____

(CT) _____

(NJ) John Berkeley, 1664

(NJ) George Carteret, 1664

(DE) _____

(MD) _____

(NC) William Berkeley, 1729

(SC) Anthony Ashley–Cooper, 1729

(GA) _____

Name: _____

Unit 4 Lesson 2
The Thirteen Colonies

Directions: Complete the chart below by organizing what you have learned about the original thirteen colonies.

	Colony	Year	Early Leaders	Reasons For Founding
NEW ENGLAND COLONIES	New Hampshire	1729	John Wheelwright	
	Massachusetts			
	Rhode Island			
	Connecticut			
MIDDLE COLONIES	New York			
	New Jersey	1664	John Berkeley George Carteret	
	Pennsylvania			
	Delaware			
SOUTHERN COLONIES	Maryland			
	Virginia			
	North Carolina	1653	William Berkeley	
	South Carolina	1670	Anthony Ashley-Cooper	
	Georgia			

Name: _____

Who founded the colonies and why?

1. Compare and Contrast: Fill in the chart below to show how the reasons for founding the New England, Middle, and Southern Colonies were alike and how they were different.

Reasons for Founding New England, Middle, and Southern Colonies

Alike	**Different**

2. *Recall* List the three types of colonies England formed in North America in the late 1500s and 1600s.

_____

_____

3. *Analyze* Many of the Southern Colonies were founded as proprietary colonies. What drew proprietors to this area? How did they make money?

_____

_____

4. *Evaluate* People of all backgrounds were invited to live in colonial Pennsylvania, free from **persecution.** How do you think that affected religious practices in the colony? Explain your answer.

_____

_____

5. **Write a Plan** Suppose you want to found your own colony. Write a plan explaining your reasons for wanting to found it. Discuss the benefits to the people who move there.

Link to ⚭ **Visual Arts** Suppose you are a founder of one of the colonies. Create a poster to attract settlers to your colony.

Lesson 2 Assessment

Answers

1.

Reasons for founding New England, Middle, and Southern Colonies

gain wealth by owning land and from natural resources to escape religious persecution or intolerance	offered a new start for debtors started as trading posts
Alike	**Different**

2. Corporate colonies, proprietary colonies, and royal colonies

3. Proprietors came to this area because of its rich soil and good harbors. They made money by establishing plantations.

4. Possible answer: There were probably many different religions practiced in Pennsylvania because people were free to choose their religion.

5. Students' plans should clearly explain why the colony is being founded and present the benefits of living there. Use the following persuasive writing rubric to score students' plans:

4	Student writes a multiple-paragraph persuasive composition that describes both sound reasons and benefits. Spelling and grammar are correct.
3	Student writes one or two paragraphs that describe some reasons and benefits. Spelling and grammar may have a few errors.
2	Student writes a one-paragraph persuasive composition that describes some reasons but may not include benefits. Spelling and grammar have some serious errors.
1	Student writes a persuasive composition that is not organized as a paragraph. It describes few or no reasons or benefits. There are many serious errors.

Link to ∞ Visual Arts Students' posters should present visuals and text that highlight the colony's benefits.

Intervention

Reading Skill Mini-Lesson ELA 5RC2.1

Direct students to review pp. 73–75. Remind them to look for signal words such as *alike* and *different*. Then ask them to reread the chart on p. 76 for more details on the similarities and differences in reasons for founding the colonies.

Analysis Skill Mini-Lesson HI 3

Ask students how allowing people of all religions and backgrounds to live together could lead to religious and cultural tolerance. Ask: *What do you think would have been the effect on our nation if each colony had only accepted people of the same background and religion?*

Writing Skill Mini-Lesson ELA 5WA2.4

Tell students that good persuasive writing contains sound reasons. Ask students to cite reasons the early colonists founded their colonies. Then ask them to brainstorm reasons they might have for founding their ideal colony in the twenty-first century. Have them talk about the kind of people who might settle the colony, and what specific benefits they would have. Ask them to compare the two. What would they have in common? What would be their major differences?

Visual Arts Support VAPA VA2.7

Direct students to show visuals of people and life in the colonies.

How did religion affect the founding of the colonies?

 California Objective H-SS 5.4.3 Describe the religious aspects of the earliest colonies (e.g., Puritanism in Massachusetts, Anglicanism in Virginia, Catholicism in Maryland, Quakerism in Pennsylvania).

STANDARDS TRACE	
Introduce	Reinforce
pp. **77**T4, **77–80**	pp. **80**T1–T5

Content Paths

✓ Core Instruction	Alternate Instruction	
△ Text Path, p. **77**T4 Student Text, pp. **77–80** Biography: Anne Hutchinson	📝 **Digital Path,** p. **80**T1 Video: *Religion and the Colonies*	✋ **Active Path,** pp. **80**T2–T4 *Colonial Williamsburg* Activity: Examine Biographies

Big Ideas

Students Will Learn

Puritans established the colony of Massachusetts.

Teacher Background

Puritan towns were carefully planned. At the center of the town was a building called a "meeting house," where town meetings and religious services were held. The Puritans believed in education. They especially wanted children to learn how to read the Bible for themselves and understand the laws of the community. Although the Puritans of Massachusetts appreciated their freedom of religion, they did not extend that freedom to others.

Common Misconception: Many students may think that freedom of religion has always existed in the United States. Explain to students that while all colonies had laws about religious tolerance, these laws were not always observed.

Anglicanism was the official religion in Virginia. Maryland was founded by Catholics.

The first Lord Baltimore, George Calvert of England, converted to Catholicism after working in Ireland for the king. He started to serve in Parliament in 1609. However, because England was Anglican, he had to resign from Parliament. King James I compensated him with land in Baltimore, Ireland, making him Lord Baltimore. James also gave Calvert a land grant in Virginia, but when he sailed to Jamestown he was not allowed to settle there because he was Catholic. His son Cecil, the second Lord Baltimore, set up the colony his father had planned in Maryland with a grant from King Charles I.

In Pennsylvania, Quaker William Penn established the Great Law in 1682 giving everyone in the Pennsylvania colony freedom of conscience, leading to a government based on religious tolerance.

People from many religions lived in the Middle Colonies.

The religious and linguistic diversity in Pennsylvania and other Middle Colonies created problems in establishing a common school system. Children were taught in parish or parochial schools so that religious teaching could be combined with reading and other subjects. New Netherland operated a few schools, but when the British took over the colony, the schools closed. Pennsylvania made plans to open public schools, but hostility between religious groups interrupted the project. In 1701 these groups decided to maintain the parochial school system.

Reading Transparency R16

Make Generalizations Use the transparency before teaching the lesson to generalize that *some religious groups became intolerant of religious practices different from their own beliefs.*

Prefixes Adding *in-* to the listed words makes the words *intolerant* and *inseparable.* Other *in-* words include *insensitive* and *insignificant.*

Audio Student Text

digital ◀)) A digital audio version of the Student Text is available for students needing auditory support.

Introduce Lesson Vocabulary

For definition, see p. 77. Read and discuss the word together. Have students use a thesaurus to find synonyms and antonyms for *intolerant* such as *harsh, strict,* and *unforgiving* (synonyms) and *patient, relaxed,* and *open-minded* (antonyms).

intolerant

Assessment

digital Lesson Pretest

• Ongoing Assessment pp. **77**T4, **80**T1, **80**T2

• Lesson Assessment p. **80**T6

digital Lesson Quiz

Universal Access

English Learners

The Role of Religion Help students understand the role of religion in the founding of the colonies.

Beginning (Level 1): On the board, provide students with details such as "Roger Williams founded Rhode Island" and "Lord Baltimore founded Maryland." Then have them determine a main idea that unifies the details.

Intermediate (Levels 2–3): Have students create a three-column chart with the headings "New England," "Middle," and "Southern." Then have students write the main religions of each region in the appropriate column.

Advanced (Levels 4–5): Have students suppose they are living in the colonies. Have them write a letter to a friend in Europe explaining religious freedom in the colonies.

digital ◀)) Audio Student Text

Extra Support

Make Generalizations Ask students to make generalizations about religion and religious freedom in the New England, Southern, and Middle Colonies.

Compare and Contrast Have students compare and contrast the religious beliefs of the three colonial regions by completing a two-column chart labeled "Common Beliefs" and "Differing Beliefs."

digital ◀)) Audio Student Text

Inclusion/Special Needs

Extend Conversation Lead a discussion about the definition of *tolerance* and why it is important. Ask students what kinds of things we can do at home, at school, and in the community to show tolerance. Make a list of specific examples of tolerant behaviors on the board.

Expand Vocabulary Discuss the relationship between the words *tolerant* and *intolerant.* Help students identify words whose opposite can be formed with the prefix *-in* or *-un,* such as *direct, experienced,* and *considerate,* etc. Challenge students to use each pair of words in sentences that distinguish their meanings.

digital ◀)) Audio Student Text

Challenge

Extend Conversation Lead a discussion about religious freedom in the United States today. Discuss whether or not we have more religious freedom now than the colonists did and why religious freedom is such an important issue to so many people.

Research to Learn More Ask students to research the religious freedom in other countries. Ask them to give a specific example of another country where people have fled to seek religious freedom.

Path Prep

LESSON 3 How did religion affect the founding of the colonies?

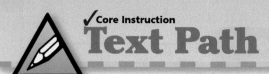 H-SS 5.4.3

Pacing	Materials	Assessment
35 MINUTES	• Student Text, pp. **77–80** • Student Text Transparencies, pp. **77–80** • *Find Out More* Handout, p. **80**T5	• **digital** Lesson Pretest • Lesson Assessment, p. **80**T6 • **digital** Lesson Quiz

1 Build Background

Activate Prior Knowledge Review with students the following terms from Lesson 2: *persecution, Separatist, pilgrim,* and *Puritan.* Have students use these terms to descibe some of the religious reasons for English colonists coming to North America.

Preview the Lesson Read *Set the Scene* with the class and note the photo of Bruton Parish Church in Williamsburg, Virginia, on p. 77. Tell students that people did not always find the religious freedom they sought. Many moved because they could not worship freely.

Introduce Vocabulary After students complete the vocabulary activity on p. 77, ask: *If a policy were described as* unofficial, *would it be approved by the government? If a person were* invisible, *could we see him or her?* Ask for other *un-* and *in-* examples. (*incomplete, incoherent, undo, unaware, uncertain, uneducated, uneasy, uneven, unfair*)

2 Teach

Read Together (pp. **78–79**) After each section, pause to discuss the lesson question "How did religion affect the founding of the colonies?" and how the section helps answer that question.

Reading Informational Text Point out to students that there are sections for each of the colonial regions. When information is organized in this way, it is often easier to identify similarities and differences in the topics.

digital ◀)) **Audio Student Text**

Summarize As they write their answers to the Lesson Summary on p. 79, point out to students that there were different effects of religion in all three of the colonial regions. Suggest using

a graphic organizer such as a three-ring Venn diagram to organize information before writing.

Biography: Anne Hutchinson (p. **80**) Read the page together. Ask students what other colonies Hutchinson might have moved to in order to practice her religion freely. Use the Student Text Transparency to help students complete the study questions.

Ongoing *Assessment* ★

▶ **IF** students have difficulty locating the reasons people left the Massachusetts Bay colony (Question 2),

▶ **THEN** point out that sometimes a cause can be the main idea of a paragraph, with effects as supporting details.

3 Assess and Extend

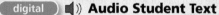

Lesson Assessment (p. **80**T6)

Extend Ask students to identify how the narrative is written to emphasize the importance of religion to the Pilgrims in the read-aloud book, *The Pilgrims of Plimoth.*

Find Out More (p. **80**T5) Have students read the page. Ask them to recall how they first learned to read and write, then have a class discussion about any similarities or differences.

Name:

H-SS 5.4.3 Describe the religious aspects of the earliest colonies (e.g., Puritanism in Massachusetts, Anglicanism in Virginia, Catholicism in Maryland, Quakerism in Pennsylvania).

Unit 4 • Life in the Colonies

Lesson 3

How did religion affect the founding of the colonies?

SET THE SCENE One thing many early colonists had in common was a strong religious faith. However, the colonists practiced religion in different ways.

Preview the Lesson
Vocabulary

intolerant *(adj.)* to be not accepting of ideas or behaviors different from one's own

Vocabulary Activity The prefixes *in-* and *un-* mean "not." Circle the prefix in the vocabulary word above. Then write a definition for the root word based on what you know about the meaning of the prefix.

accepting of ideas or behaviors different from one's own

People
Anne Hutchinson

Reading: Make Generalizations

Remember that to *make generalizations* you use facts from a text to write statements that are true most of the time. As you read the first paragraph on page 78, place check marks next to sentences that contains facts about religious laws in the colonies.

77

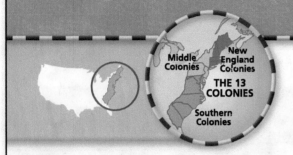

Religion in the Colonies

You have learned that some people came to North America to find a place to worship freely. ✔ In fact, every colony had laws that officially allowed freedom of religion. However, most colonies had established churches too. An established church is a religious group that is supported by the government. ✔ Laws said that even people who did not belong to this group had to pay taxes to support it. The conflict between religious freedom and established churches played a key role in the development of some colonies.

The New England Puritans

The colony of Massachusetts began as a place for Puritans to practice their religion freely. However, only Puritan church members could vote and church leaders called ministers held a lot of power. Some of these leaders were **intolerant,** or to be not accepting of ideas or behaviors different from their own.

People who disagreed with Puritan leaders began to leave Massachusetts. Thomas Hooker, a minister, did not agree that only church members should rule. He left the colony and founded Hartford, which later became part of the colony of Connecticut. Roger Williams was forced to leave Massachusetts for his beliefs too. As a result, he founded the colony of Rhode Island, whose charter stated that no one could be punished "for any differences in opinion in matters of religion." Anne Hutchinson also challenged the power of Puritan leaders when she began leading her own religious meetings. Like Williams, Hutchinson was forced to leave the colony and moved to Rhode Island.

78 • Life in the Colonies

1. ◉ Make Generalizations **Underline a sentence in the text that makes a generalization about the role of religion in the development of the colonies.**

2. **What caused people to leave the Massachusetts Bay colony?**
   Cause and Effect

   ✎ Disagreements with Puritan leaders caused people such as Thomas Hooker, Roger Williams, and Anne Hutchinson to leave the colony.

After disagreements with Puritan leaders in Massachusetts, Roger Williams received a charter to start the colony of Rhode Island.

Religion in the Southern Colonies

Established churches played an important role in the Southern Colonies too. Anglicanism, or the Church of England, was the established church of Virginia. John Smith recalled that, from the earliest days, "[We] had daily Common Prayer morning and evening, every Sunday two Sermons." Lord Baltimore founded Maryland as a place where Catholics who were persecuted in England could live in peace. However, many non-Catholics also moved there, and leaders soon passed a law giving religious freedom to all Christians.

Religion in the Middle Colonies

Unlike the other colonial regions, people from many religions lived in the Middle Colonies. People from a variety of countries, cultures, and religions settled in the colony of New York. Pennsylvania and Delaware did not have established churches, so people from many different religious groups settled there too. In Pennsylvania a group called the Quakers welcomed people of all religions and backgrounds. The Quakers believed in leading a simple life. <u>They preferred simple styles of clothing and buildings and opposed war and other acts of violence.</u>

3. How was the founding of Maryland like the founding of Rhode Island? *Compare and Contrast*

✎ These colonies were both founded as places where people could practice their religion more freely.

_____

_____

_____

4. Underline a sentence that gives details about the beliefs of Pennsylvania Quakers.

Main Idea and Details

Quakers "go to meeting" but have no regular services or ministers. Instead, they believe people should pray in a way that feels right to them.

Summary Answer In New England, Puritans founded Massachusetts as a place to worship freely, but conflicts with the established church led people to found new colonies. The Southern Colony of Virginia had an established church, but Maryland welcomed all Christians. Middle Colonies such as Pennsylvania and New York had people from many faiths.

Summary

Religion was an important part of life in the English colonies. Describe the effect of religion in the three colonial regions.

Unit 4 Lesson 3 • 79

LESSON 3
Overview

LESSON 3
Text Path

LESSON 3
Digital Path

LESSON 3
Active Path

LESSON 3
Assessment

Biography

Anne Hutchinson, 1591–1643

Learn More Anne Hutchinson spent her life in pursuit of religious freedom. Her religious beliefs were greatly influenced by a minister named John Cotton and by her father, who was also a minister. Hutchinson's father was not afraid to speak his mind. <u>He was twice sent to prison in England for speaking out against the Church of England. In 1633 John Cotton was forced to leave England because of his beliefs.</u> Hutchinson and her family followed Cotton to Boston.

In Boston, Hutchinson spoke freely about her beliefs. She held meetings in her home, where she taught that faith was more important than following the rules of the established church. Some colonial leaders disapproved of Hutchinson's beliefs. They took her to court, and she was forced to leave the colony. She moved first to Rhode Island, which had been founded on the promise of religious freedom, and later to New York. The risks taken by Hutchinson and others like her helped establish the freedom of religion in the United States today.

Answer the questions below.

1. Underline the events in Hutchinson's father's life and in John Cotton's life that taught her about standing up for her beliefs. *Identify*

2. Why do you think church leaders disapproved of Hutchinson's actions?

Interpret

Possible answer: Hutchinson taught people that faith was more important than following the rules of the established church.

80 • Life in the Colonies

Digital Path

LESSON 3 How did religion affect the founding of the colonies?

🐻 H-SS 5.4.3

Path Prep	**Pacing**	**Materials**	**Assessment**
	50 MINUTES	· Video: *Religion and the Colonies* · Interactive Practice: *Different Religions, Different Colonies* · Print Partner: *Religion Affects Settlement* · digital ◀)) Audio Student Text	· digital Lesson Pretest · Lesson Assessment, p. **80** T6 · digital Lesson Quiz

1 Build Background

Activate Prior Knowledge Have students share what they learned in the previous lesson about the role religious persecution in Europe played in the initial settlement of North America. Explain that in this lesson, they will learn that religion continued to be a powerful force in the colonies as they grew.

Introduce Vocabulary Introduce the lesson vocabulary word using the print or digital card.

Lesson Introduction Launch the Lesson Introduction, which asks the question, "How did religion affect the founding of the colonies?"

2 Teach

Video As students view *Religion and the Colonies,* have them consider these questions:
• Why were Hartford and Rhode Island founded?
• What part did religion play in the establishment of the Maryland Colony?
• Why were the Middle Colonies home to people of many different religions?

Interactive Practice Launch *Different Religions, Different Colonies.* The activity will help students understand that religion was a key factor in the founding of the colonies.

Print Partner Have students complete the Print Partner. In the activity, students will

explain how religion influenced the founding of the colonies.

 ◀)) **Audio Student Text**

Ongoing *Assessment* ★

▶ **IF** students are struggling to understand why people from different religions were welcomed in the Middle Colonies,

▶ **THEN** remind students that Pennsylvania, a large part of the Middle Colonies, was settled by Quakers, who welcomed all religious groups. Add that New York City, one of the largest cities in the Middle Colonies, had historically accommodated people of various ethnic and religious backgrounds.

3 Assess and Extend

digital Lesson Quiz Have students check their understanding of the lesson content by answering the questions. After students finish the page, review the answers with the class.

Lesson Assessment Use the assessment on p. **80** T6 to evaluate students' lesson comprehension.

Extend Organize the class into two groups. Have one group research the Puritans of the Massachusetts Colony, the other group, the Quakers of the Pennsylvania Colony. On a bulletin board, draw a large Venn diagram. Have students record facts about their religious group on the diagram. Then have students work together to fill in the center column with characteristics shared by the religious groups.

LESSON 3
Overview

LESSON 3
Text Path

LESSON 3
Digital Path

LESSON 3
Active Path

LESSON 3
Assessment

Alternate Instruction
Active Path

Colonial Williamsburg

LESSON 3 How did religion affect the founding of the colonies?

H-SS 5.4.3

Description: Students will examine biographies of religious leaders to identify some religious aspects of the early colonies.

Path Prep

Pacing

50 MINUTES

Materials
- *Big Book Atlas*, transparency and markers
- Biography Cards, pp. **96** T23–T26 (picture side only) for each person discussed in this lesson
- Handouts, pp. **80** T3–T4

Assessment
- digital Lesson Pretest
- Lesson Assessment, p. **80** T6
- digital Lesson Quiz

1 Build Background

Activate Prior Knowledge Using p. 111 of the *Big Book Atlas,* have students review the names of the colonies and the major reasons they were founded. Be certain that students mention the desire for freedom of religion.

Introduce Vocabulary Conduct a discussion introducing the vocabulary word *intolerant.* Ask: *What problems do you think intolerance might cause? Why?*

2 Teach

Introduce Activity Explain to students that they will read brief biographies of some early colonists who sought religious freedom. Using that information, they will respond to the following questions (written on the board): *What different religions are represented in the biographical sketches? What are some specific features of each religion?*

Activity Steps

1. Divide the class into six groups and give each group one biography from the *Biographies of Religious Leaders* handouts. After each group has read and answered the questions, discuss as a class the answers to the questions for each biography. Ask how the biographies help us understand the impact of religion on the founding of the colonies.

2. Prepare a transparency of a map of the thirteen colonies. Create a legend at the

bottom of the map *(Puritan, Anglican, Catholic, Quaker,* and *Religiously Free)* and assign one color to each religion. Display the transparency for students. As a class, determine which religion(s) were associated with each colony. Color or crosshatch each colony accordingly. [Note: If you would like to show the students pictures of the individuals, show them the Biography Cards, images from pp. **96** T23–T26.]

Ongoing *Assessment* ★

▶ **IF** students have difficulty with the concept of a state- or colony-wide, church,

▶ **THEN** ask them to think about the reasons some colonists came to North America. Remind them that there was no tradition of religious tolerance where they came from.

3 Assess and Extend

Assess Ask students to write a two-sentence summary of the role of religion in the founding of the colonies.

Lesson Assessment (p. **80** T6)

Extend Have students create a time line of the founding of the colonies discussed in this lesson.

Biographies of Religious Leaders 1

William Bradford

As a boy, William Bradford went to Puritan church meetings. These Puritans were also called Separatists and believed the Anglican Church (England's official state church) should not tell them how to worship. Because the Separatists wanted to select their own minister and choose their own form of worship, they moved to Amsterdam in the Netherlands to escape the control of the church. William Bradford went with them. William Bradford helped organize the Pilgrims' move to the colonies. He became the governor of the new colony called Plymouth. What colony did William Bradford help found?

William Penn

William Penn joined the Society of Friends in 1667. Members of the Society of Friends were also called Quakers. They believed that church and state should be separate. They also were against war and the taking of oaths. William Penn was put in jail several times because of his religious opinions. In 1681 King Charles II of England gave William Penn a large piece of land in North America as payment for a debt owed to Penn's father. The next year, Penn traveled to North America and established a new colony. He built his colony on Quaker beliefs. He named the colony after his father. What colony is named for William Penn?

Cecilius Calvert, Second Lord Baltimore

Cecilius Calvert was a Roman Catholic. Most English people were Anglican, not Roman Catholic. They were afraid of Catholics and treated them poorly. The King of England, Charles I, gave the Calvert family a large piece of land in North America, north of the Potomac River. Calvert sent settlers to his new colony. In 1634 about two hundred settlers arrived, including two Catholic priests and many other Catholics. Calvert wanted Catholics and Anglicans to live together in his colony. A city in this colony was named after him. What colony did Cecilius Calvert found?

Biographies of Religious Leaders 2

Roger Williams

Roger Williams went to the Massachusetts Bay Colony in 1631. He was a minister, but he also believed that religion and government were separate. He spoke out about these beliefs and the Massachusetts government forced him to leave the colony. In 1636 he moved and started a new colony. He founded the city of Providence and started the first Baptist Church in North America. In this new colony, Roger Williams established religious freedom. What colony did Roger Williams found?

Anne Hutchinson

Anne Hutchinson and her family moved from England to Boston, Massachusetts, in 1634. She held religious meetings in her home. Hutchinson became popular. Her teachings threatened the authority of the Massachusetts church and government. She was tried by the General Court and forced to leave Massachusetts in 1638. She moved to a new colony immediately south of Massachusetts that had religious freedom. Where did Anne Hutchinson move after she was forced to leave Massachusetts? What was this new colony's name?

Thomas Hooker

Thomas Hooker was a Puritan. As a Puritan, he disagreed with England's official church, the Anglican Church. The King of England was the leader of the church and had almost unlimited powers. The Puritans, however, did not believe kings made good religious leaders. Hooker first left England for the Netherlands, then moved to Massachusetts in 1633. Finally he and his congregation moved to another colony and settled the town of Hartford three years later. Hooker was well educated and became a major government and religious leader in the colony. He helped write a set of laws called the Fundamental Orders in 1639. Where did Thomas Hooker and his congregation settle? What was this colony's name?

Unit 4 Lesson 3

Religion in Colonial America

As you have read, religion was important in the colonies. It was so important that children in New England learned to read by reading the Bible.

Many children in the New England Colonies first learned to read using something called the "hornbook." The hornbook was a board shaped like a paddle. On the board was a piece of paper. At the top of the paper was a cross. Next came the alphabet. Beneath the alphabet was *The Lord's Prayer*.

In 1690 a schoolbook called the *New England Primer* was published. This book taught children to read using pictures and rhymes about the Bible. It also had prayers and stories from the Bible.

A hornbook (left) and a page from the *New England Primer* (below)

Name: _____

How did religion affect the founding of the colonies?

1. 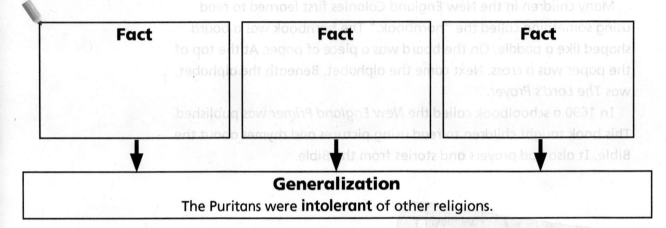 **Make Generalizations:** Fill in the chart below with three facts that lead to the generalization.

Fact	Fact	Fact

Generalization

The Puritans were **intolerant** of other religions.

2. *Understand* How did religious intolerance in the Massachusetts Bay Colony lead to the founding of other New England colonies?

_____

_____

3. *Analyze* Explain why the Middle Colonies were more accepting of other religions.

_____

_____

4. *Evaluate* Do you think the founders of the colonies discussed in the lesson reached their goals for religious freedom? Explain your answer.

_____

_____

5. **Write Research-Based Paragraphs** Write a short research report that compares and contrasts attitudes about religion in the Middle Colonies with those in the New England Colonies. Remember to include specific facts and details.

Link to ⚭ Geography Using the map handout of "The Thirteen Colonies," show which colonies had established churches and which ones allowed colonists to practice other religions. Label as many of the religions practiced in each colony as possible.

Lesson 3 Assessment

Answers

1.

Fact	Fact	Fact
Some of the colony's leaders were intolerant of other people's religious ideas.	Only church members could vote.	Church leaders called ministers held a great deal of power.

Generalization
The Puritans were intolerant of other religions.

2. People who disagreed with the Puritans left Massachusetts and founded other colonies where they could practice their beliefs.

3. People from different backgrounds, cultures, and religions settled in the Middle Colonies, so the people in these colonies were more understanding of other people's differences.

4. Students' answers should include the fact that some founders, like the Puritans, were not tolerant of other people's religions, while others, like the Quakers, welcomed people of all religions.

5. Students' paragraphs should compare the intolerant views of the Puritans in New England and the tolerant attitudes in the Middle Colonies. Use the following reasearch report rubric to score students' writing:

4	Student writes a report with well-detailed comparisons and contrasts. Spelling and grammar are correct.
3	Student writes a report with some comparisons and contrasts. Spelling and grammar may have a few errors.
2	Student writes a report with few comparisons and contrasts. Spelling and grammar have some serious errors.
1	Student writes a report with descriptions but little or no comparisons or contrasts. There are many serious errors.

Link to ⊶ Geography Students' maps should accurately show the thirteen colonies and label the colonies that had established churches and those that did not.

Intervention

Reading Skill Mini-Lesson ELA 5RC2.4
Ask students to reread the first paragraph of "The New England Puritans" on p. 78. Remind them to look for facts that have something in common and that support the generalization that the Puritans were intolerant of other religions.

Analysis Skill Mini-Lesson HI 3
Help students understand the concept that the present is connected with the past. Explain that although some groups (the Puritans) came to America seeking religious freedom, they became intolerant of others' faith and forced these people to leave their colony. These people went on to establish new religious practices and new colonies.

Writing Skill Mini-Lesson ELA 5WA2.3
Tell students that a good research report establishes a topic, important ideas, and details. Ask students to help you list the attitudes toward religion people had in the Middle Colonies and in the New England Colonies. From this list, help them see what these colonists had in common and what their differences were.

Geography Support H-SS 5.4.3
Give students the map on p. **76**T4 and provide resources about the religions in each colony.

How did the First Great Awakening affect the colonies?

California Objective H-SS 5.4.4 Identify the significance and leaders of the First Great Awakening, which marked a shift in religious ideas, practices, and allegiances in the colonial period, the growth of religious toleration, and free exercise of religion.

STANDARDS TRACE	
Introduce	Reinforce
pp. **81** T4, **81–84**	pp. **84** T1–T5, **102**

✓ Core Instruction

Content Paths

Text Path, p. 81 T4
Student Text, pp. **81–84**
Skill: Circle Graphs

Alternate Instruction

Digital Path, p. 84 T1
Video: *The First Great Awakening*

Active Path, pp. 84 T2-T4
Colonial Williamsburg
Activity: Primary Sources of the Great Awakening

Big Ideas

Students Will Learn

Religious changes occurred in the colonies in the early 1700s.

George Whitefield was an important leader of the First Great Awakening.

Some people embraced the First Great Awakening, while others resisted it.

Teacher Background

In the 1700s, many Christian leaders helped their congregations experience a new kind of emotional relationship with their religion. This period is called the Great Awakening. In colonial America, the First Great Awakening was followed by a second from 1790 until the 1830s, which produced increased church attendance and demands for social reforms such as women's rights and the abolition of slavery.

Common Misconception: Students may think that the Great Awakening was a unique event in history. Explain that there have been many revivals in Christianity for many centuries, for example, the Crusades, the Reformation, and the Counter Reformation.

The First Great Awakening started in England and spread to the colonies. George Whitefield was an Anglican deacon from Gloucester, England. He was influenced by John and Charles Wesley, the founders of Methodism. At the time, Methodism was only a movement within the Anglican church, and "methodist" had been just a nickname reflecting their methodical ways. The Wesleys traveled widely in England to bring their message to the masses and Whitefield followed their example, going to Georgia to preach. But Anglican clergy did not allow Whitefield to preach in their churches because of his Methodist connections so he began holding informal revival meetings. Many colleges and universities were founded as a result of the Great Awakening, such as Princeton in New Jersey and the University of Pennsylvania.

The formation of the Baptist church during the First Great Awakening led to the growth of many new Baptist groups. Roger Williams started the spread of the Baptist faith in Providence in 1639, but the Baptist community did not gain much strength until the formation of the Philadelphia Baptist Association in 1707. In the South, Baptists remained separate from the traditional Baptist groups longer than those in the New England colonies. Then in 1758, a new, more emotional style of Baptist church appeared. Throughout the 1800s, the establishment of African American Baptist churches in the South grew significantly. Many of these churches have served as centers of African American communities.

Reading Transparency R17

Main Idea and Details Use the transparency to reinforce identifying details about the main idea: *Religion played an important role in the lives of American Colonists.*

Suffixes Ask students to identify the root word *preach,* and the suffix *-er.*

Audio Student Text

(digital) ◀)) A digital audio version of the Student Text is available for students needing auditory support.

Introduce Lesson Vocabulary

For definition, see p. 81. Read the word and definition together. Ask students to find additional words that have the *-er* suffix that means "one who does something" such as *teacher, farmer,* and *leader.*

preacher

(digital) Lesson Pretest

• Ongoing Assessment pp. **81** T4, **84** T1, **84** T2

• Lesson Assessment p. **84** T6

(digital) Lesson Quiz

English Learners

Religious Changes Help students understand the impact of the Great Awakening.

Beginning (Level 1): Use the circle graph on p. 84 as you model comparing and contrasting. Say: *There are more Baptists than Methodists. There are fewer Lutherans than Methodists.* Have students use the graph as they form their own sentences.

Intermediate (Levels 2–3): As a group, have students come up with a list of changes that occured as a result of the Great Awakening.

Advanced (Levels 4–5): Have students write a short speech about something they feel strongly about changing. Have them share and relate their speeches to the Great Awakening.

(digital) ◀)) Audio Student Text

Extra Support

Identify Cause and Effect Tell students to list each of the following as causes in a cause-and-effect chart: *people questioned importance of religion, revivals, George Whitefield holds revivals.* Have them complete their charts by identifying the effects of each.

Make Generalizations Ask students to make generalizations about what brought about the First Great Awakening and how it affected the colonies.

(digital) ◀)) Audio Student Text

Inclusion/Special Needs

Use Key Words Write each of the following words or phrases on the board: *people doubted importance of religion, revivals, increased interest in religion, new religions emerged.* Help students identify key words or phrases from the lesson that are associated with each. Write their responses on the board and use the chart to discuss the effect of the First Great Awakening.

Extend Conversation Discuss with students the many Christian denominations that exist today, particularly those whose roots can be traced back to the First Great Awakening, such as Baptists and Methodists.

(digital) ◀)) Audio Student Text

Challenge

Evaluate Ask students why they think people began to question the importance of religion back in the 1700s. Ask them to consider what life was like for the colonists and the reasons they first came to the colonies.

Compare and Contrast Lead a discussion comparing the revivals of the First Great Awakening to the religious movements today. Discuss how modern technology has changed how preachers reach their followers and how it affects their ability to attract and maintain members.

LESSON 4
Overview

LESSON 4
Text Path

LESSON 4
Digital Path

LESSON 4
Active Path

LESSON 4
Assessment

LESSON 4 How did the First Great Awakening affect the colonies?

🐻 H-SS 5.4.4

| Path Prep | Pacing 35 MINUTES | Materials · Student Text, pp. **81–84** · Student Text Transparencies, pp. **81–84** · *Find Out More* Handout, p. **84**T5 | Assessment · digital Lesson Pretest · Lesson Assessment, p. **84**T6 · digital Lesson Quiz |

---

1 Build Background

Activate Prior Knowledge Explain to students that many people change their beliefs, investigate new ways of thinking or believing, or alter or expand their basic beliefs over their lifetimes. Similarly, as time went by and they were exposed to new ways of thinking, some American colonists began to change their ideas about religion and began practicing religion in new ways.

Preview the Lesson Read *Set the Scene* with the class. Have students study the picture and describe what seems to be going on. Tell students they will read that during the 1700s people developed new types of religions according to new ideas.

Introduce Vocabulary After students complete the vocabulary activity on p. 81, ask what they would call someone who leads *(leader)*. What would they call a person who believes? *(believer)*

---

2 Teach

Read Together (pp. **82–83**) Remind students of the religious intolerence of early colonial times. After each section, pause to discuss how the Great Awakening changed this.

Reading Informational Text Read the excerpt from Jonathan Edwards's letter on p. 82. Ask what this quote tells us about Edwards's viewpoint on the effects of the Great Awakening.

digital ◀)) **Audio Student Text**

Summarize Remind students that as they answer the Lesson Summary on p. 83 they should include more than one way religious practices changed during this period.

Skill: Circle Graphs CST 3 (p. **84**) Read the skill page together. Ask students what religions they recognize from the graph. Ask what the graph shows about religious diversity in the United States.

Ongoing *Assessment* ★

▶ **IF** students have difficulty locating the sentences that give them the main ideas of the Great Awakening (Question 2),

▶ **THEN** remind them that the main idea is usually stated in the topic sentence, which is often the first sentence of a paragraph.

---

3 Assess and Extend

Lesson Assessment (p. **84**T6)

Extend The circle graph on p. 84 is based on a survey population of 207,980,000. Based on the percentages, have students calculate the totals for each religion.

Find Out More (p. **84**T5) Have students read the page, then separate into groups to discuss the questions. Have them write a few sentences that reflect their group's comments, and then share these sentences with the class.

Name:

🐻 **H-SS 5.4.4** Identify the significance and leaders of the First Great Awakening, which marked a shift in religious ideas, practices, and allegiances in the colonial period, the growth of religious toleration, and free exercise of religion.

Unit 4 • Life in the Colonies
Lesson 4

How did the First Great Awakening affect the colonies?

SET THE SCENE Have you ever changed the way you thought about something? Ideas and beliefs can change over time. In the 1700s, many colonists began to change how they thought about religion. These changes led colonists to practice their religion in new ways.

Preview the Lesson
Vocabulary

preacher *(n.)* a person who gives speeches about religious subjects

Vocabulary Activity As you know, the suffix *-er* means "one who." For example, a *teacher* is one who teaches. Circle the suffix in the vocabulary word above. Then write a definition for the root word below.

preach *(v.)* to give a speech on a religious subject

People
Jonathan Edwards
George Whitefield

Reading: Main Idea and Details

A *main idea* is a statement that tells you what a paragraph is generally about. *Details* can be found in sentences that support or explain the main idea. As you read the second paragraph on page 82, circle the names of three people that support the paragraph's main idea. ▷

81

LESSON 4
Overview

LESSON 4
Text Path

LESSON 4
Digital Path

LESSON 4
Active Path

LESSON 4
Assessment

1730   1735

1734 Jonathan Edwards starts religious revivals in New England.

Religious Changes in the Colonies

As you have learned, religion was an important part of many American colonists' lives. However, in the 1730s, some Protestants began to develop new ideas about religion. They wanted religion to be about strong emotions that could be felt by anybody instead of about difficult ideas that were understood by few people. This was the beginning of a period known as the First Great Awakening.

The First Great Awakening

The First Great Awakening spread throughout the colonies. In 1734 Jonathan Edwards began holding religious meetings called revivals in New England. At revivals, preachers gave emotional speeches warning people about the dangers of a weak faith. A **preacher** is a person who gives speeches about religious subjects. In the Middle Colonies, Gilbert Tennent and his family held large revivals. Samuel Davies brought this new kind of religious service to the Southern Colonies in 1748.

One of the most important people in the First Great Awakening was a traveling preacher from Britain named George Whitefield (WIT feeld). In 1739 Whitefield began traveling throughout the colonies. He often preached in open fields to large crowds. These crowds often contained a wide variety of people, including men, women, and children, rich and poor, and members of different religions. Many of these people felt more strongly about their faith after hearing Whitefield speak. He also inspired many new preachers, who imitated his dramatic speaking style.

1. How did some colonists' ideas about religion begin to change?

Main Idea and Details

They wanted religion to be about strong emotions instead of difficult ideas.

2. In the text, underline the sentence in each paragraph that gives the main idea.

Main Idea and Details

"Ever since the great work of God [a revival] that was wrought [happened] here . . . there has been a great abiding [lasting] alteration [change] in this town in many respects. There has been vastly more religion kept up in the town, among all sorts of persons, in religious exercises and in common conversation than used to be before."

— Jonathan Edwards, in a letter dated December 12, 1743

82 • Life in the Colonies

1740   1745   1750

1739
George Whitefield begins preaching tours of the colonies.

1748 Samuel Davies brings revivals to the Southern Colonies.

Effects of the Great Awakening

The First Great Awakening increased many colonists' interest in religion. However, some people disagreed with the changes it brought. Many Puritans did not agree with these new ideas. Among a group called the Presbyterians, colonists split into groups called "old lights," who disagreed with the revivals, and "new lights," who favored them.

Despite this resistance, the First Great Awakening influenced people throughout the colonies in many ways. Thousands of people joined new religious groups, such as the (Baptists) or (Methodists.) Some of these groups reached out to African Americans. Religious groups also set up many new schools, including universities that still exist today. The growth and spread of such groups led to greater acceptance of people of different faiths throughout the colonies. Many colonists also began to believe that they could stand up to authority on important issues like religion. Finally, these changes brought many colonists together behind a common set of ideas, which had a lasting effect on the role of religion and politics throughout the colonies.

3. In the text, circle two religious groups that grew as a result of the First Great Awakening.

Main Idea and Details

Princeton University and many other schools were founded by religious groups during the First Great Awakening.

Summary Answer During the First Great Awakening, people throughout the colonies began attending religious meetings called revivals. These meetings were held by religious leaders called preachers, who wanted religion to be about strong emotions. Although some people disagreed with the Awakening, it gave rise to new religious groups, increased religious toleration, and led colonists to believe they could question authority.

Summary

In the 1700s, religious ideas in the colonies began to change. How did the First Great Awakening change the way many colonists practiced their religion?

Unit 4 Lesson 4 • **83**

LESSON 4 Overview

LESSON 4 Text Path

LESSON 4 Digital Path

LESSON 4 Active Path

LESSON 4 Assessment

Skill

Circle Graphs

Learn More Circle graphs use percentages or fractions to compare information. The size of each section of the graph represents a portion of the whole. If you add the pieces together, the total will equal 100 percent.

As the population of the United States grows and changes, so does the variety of religions practiced here. The circle graph below shows some of the religions practiced in the United States based on a survey. Each section represents a part of the population that belongs to a particular religion. Use the graph to answer the questions.

Try It

1. Underline the religion that is practiced by 1.3% of the people in the United States. *Identify*

2. Circle the names of two religions that are practiced by about the same percentage of people. *Identify*

3. What is the total percent of people who practice a religion or set of beliefs other than Christianity? *Interpret*

23.5%

4. If someone chose not to practice any religion, where would they be included on this graph? *Apply*

Nonreligious

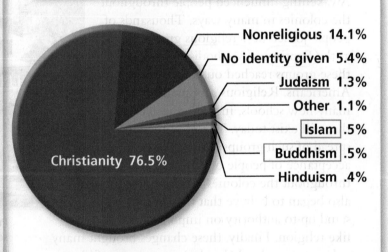

Religions in the United States

- Nonreligious 14.1%
- No identity given 5.4%
- <u>Judaism</u> 1.3%
- Other 1.1%
- Islam .5%
- Buddhism .5%
- Hinduism .4%

Christianity 76.5%

Major Christian groups:	
Catholic	24.5%
Baptist	16.3%
Methodist	6.8%
Lutheran	4.6%
Presbyterian	2.7%

Source: American Religion identity Survey, 2001

Digital Path

LESSON 4 **How did the First Great Awakening affect the colonies?** 🐻 H-SS 5.4.4

LESSON 4
Overview

LESSON 4
Text Path

LESSON 4
Digital Path

LESSON 4
Active Path

LESSON 4
Assessment

Path Prep	Pacing ⏱ 50 MINUTES	Materials • Video: *The First Great Awakening* • Interactive Practice: *"Awakening" the Colonies* • Print Partner: *Religious Changes in the Colonies* • 🔵 digital ◀)) Audio Student Text	Assessment • 🔵 digital Lesson Pretest • Lesson Assessment, p. **84**T6 • 🔵 digital Lesson Quiz

1 Build Background

Activate Prior Knowledge Begin a class discussion about the meaning of the word, *awakening*. Explain to students that they will learn about a time in American history when people "awoke" to new ideas and beliefs about religion.

Introduce Vocabulary Introduce the lesson vocabulary word using the print or digital card.

Lesson Introduction Launch the Lesson Introduction, which asks the question, "How did the First Great Awakening affect the colonies?"

2 Teach

Video As students view *The First Great Awakening,* have them consider these questions:
• In what ways did the religious practices of many Protestant groups change?
• What effects did these changes have on religion, as a whole, in the colonies?

Interactive Practice Launch the activity, *"Awakening" the Colonies.* The activity will help students understand the wide-ranging effects of the Great Awakening on the religious practices of colonial Americans.

Print Partner Ask students to complete the Print Partner activity. In the activity, students will answer questions related to how the Great

Awakening affected religious groups and their practices.

🔵 digital ◀)) **Audio Student Text**

Ongoing *Assessment* ★

▶ **IF** students are struggling to understand why the style of preaching that arose during the Great Awakening had such a strong impact on religion in the colonies,

▶ **THEN** find an excerpt from a printed text that conveys strong emotion. Read aloud the excerpt in a monotone voice; then reread it with emotion. Have students comment on their reactions to the readings. Help them recognize that a passionate reading can have great power over people.

3 Assess and Extend

🔵 digital **Lesson Quiz** Have students evaluate their understanding of the lesson content by completing the quiz. When students are finished, review the correct answers with the class.

Lesson Assessment Use the assessment on p. **84**T6 to check students' lesson comprehension.

Extend Have students brainstorm a list of the world's religions. Invite them to choose one of the religions and conduct research to learn more about it. Then have students write a script for a short documentary about the religion they studied. Set aside time for students to read aloud their scripts in class.

Active Path

Colonial Williamsburg

LESSON 4 How did the First Great Awakening affect the colonies?

🐻 H-SS 5.4.4

Description: Using primary sources, students will learn about the First Great Awakening.

Path Prep

Pacing

TWO 50-MINUTE SESSIONS

Materials
· Handouts, pp. **84**T3–T4
· Biography Cards, pp. **96**T23–T26

Assessment
· [digital] Lesson Pretest
· Lesson Assessment, p. **84**T6
· [digital] Lesson Quiz

1 Build Background

Activate Prior Knowledge Remind students that religion played an important role in the development of the colonies. Explain that in the 1730s some ministers began to develop new ways of preaching. This time is called the "First Great Awakening."

Introduce Vocabulary Go over the lesson vocabulary section found on p. 81.

2 Teach

Introduce Activity Explain to students that they will be looking at primary sources relating to George Whitefield, one of the famous preachers of the eighteenth century. Make sure they understand that Whitefield was only one of many preachers at this time.

Activity Steps

1. Give students the George Whitefield and Jonathan Edwards biography cards. Have them read the cards and describe what was happening to religion during the First Great Awakening in colonial America. You may wish to use additional reference sources. Next have students read the primary source information found on the handout.

2. Have students look carefully at *The Reverend George Whitefield* handout and describe what they see happening in the picture. Which

source do the students think better describes how Whitefield affected people?

3. Using the Whitefield handouts, have students write a narrative description of what it might have been like to see Reverend Whitefield preach. How many people came to hear? Where did he preach? What effect did he have on his audience?

Ongoing *Assessment* ★

▶ **IF** students have problems analyzing the Whitefield picture and primary source information,

▶ **THEN** ask them to reread the handout and make a list of descriptive words used in the writing. Then have students make another list of words that describe how Whitefield is depicted in the picture.

3 Assess and Extend

Assess Assessment is based on the student's narrative writing and class participation. Look for inclusion of factual details.

Lesson Assessment (p. **84**T6)

Extend Have students use library and Internet resources to make a list and write a short biography of other preachers who helped shape the Great Awakening (for example, Jonathan Edwards, Samuel Davies, John Wesley, William Tennant, and James Davenport).

 *Colonial Williamsburg*

Name: _____

Ben Franklin on George Whitefield

Directions: Read the quote below to learn what it was like to hear Reverend Whitefield preach.

Benjamin Franklin wrote:

"In 1739 arrived among us from Ireland the Reverend Mr. Whitefield, who had made himself remarkable there as an itinerant [traveling] preacher. He was at first permitted to preach in some of our churches [in Philadelphia]; but the clergy [preachers], taking a dislike to him, soon refus'd him [would not let him preach in] their pulpits, and he was oblig'd [forced] to preach in the fields. The multitudes [many people] of all sects and denominations [all the different churches] that attended his sermons were enormous. . . . It was wonderful to see the change soon made in the manners [behavior] of our inhabitants [the people of Philadelphia]. From being thoughtless or indifferent about religion, it seemed as if all the world were growing religious, so that one could not walk thro' the town in an evening without hearing psalms sung in different families of every street."

"He had a loud and clear voice, and articulated [spoke] his words and sentences so perfectly that he might be heard and understood at a great distance, especially as his auditors [people listening], however numerous, observ'd the most exact silence. . . . [I read] newspaper accounts of his having preach'd to twenty-five thousand people in the fields. . . ."

From the: *Autobiography of Benjamin Franklin*
(Boston: Houghton Mifflin & Company, 1906),
pp. 110 and 113.

Colonial Williamsburg

Name: _____

The Reverend George Whitefield

Directions: Look carefully at the picture below. Then describe what you see. What kind of person do you think Reverend Whitefield was?

The Reverend George Whitefield

_____

_____

_____

_____

_____

Name: _____

Unit 4 Lesson 4

The Great Awakening and Education

You have learned that one of the effects of the Great Awakening was to increase many colonists' interest in religion. Another effect of the Great Awakening was that it led to an increased interest in education. Part of this can be seen in the establishment of more schools and universities in the colonies during this time period. Some of our oldest colleges were started during the Great Awakening. Many were established or supported by churches or ministers.

Princeton University, established in 1746, in New Jersey, was supported by the Presbyterian Church. In New Hampshire, Dartmouth College (1769) was started by a Congregationalist minister. Rhode Island's Brown University (1764) was established during the Great Awakening. George Whitefield started a school in Philadelphia that would later become the University of Pennsylvania (1757).

Discuss the following topics with a partner or group: How might learning to read increase a person's interest in religion? How might churches benefit from more colleges and better-educated people? Use the space below to summarize your discussions for each.

_____

_____

_____

_____

_____

_____

_____

_____

_____

_____

_____

© Pearson Scott Foresman

Name: _____

How did the First Great Awakening affect the colonies?

1. Main Idea and Details: Complete the chart below by writing details that support the main idea.

Main Idea

The First Great Awakening led to changes in colonial society.

↑　　　　　　↑　　　　　　↑

Detail　　　　　**Detail**　　　　　**Detail**

2. *Recall* What was the First Great Awakening?

_____

_____

3. *Analyze* How did the First Great Awakening spread throughout the colonies?

_____

_____

4. *Synthesize* The First Great Awakening had an effect on tolerance for all people in the colonies. What do you think the colonies would have been like if this movement had not happened? Explain your answer.

_____

_____

_____

_____

5. **Write a Letter** Suppose you attended a revival meeting held by a **preacher** during the First Great Awakening. Write a letter to a pen pal in another colony describing the revival, including the setting and the reaction from the crowd.

Link to ──∞── Visual Arts Design a flier that advertises an upcoming visit by George Whitefield or Jonathan Edwards during the First Great Awakening.

Lesson 4 Assessment

Answers

LESSON 4
Overview

LESSON 4
Text Path

LESSON 4
Digital Path

LESSON 4
Active Path

LESSON 4
Assessment

1.

Main Idea

The First Great Awakening led to changes in colonial society.

↑ ↑ ↑

Thousands joined new religious groups.	There was much greater acceptance of people of different religions.	People felt empowered to stand up to authority on issues like religion.
Detail	**Detail**	**Detail**

2. It was a new way Protestant ministers practiced their religion. It was about strong emotions felt by many rather than about difficult ideas understood by only a few.

3. It was spread by religious meetings called revivals.

4. Possible answer: If the First Great Awakening had not happened, people might have remained intolerant of other people's religion. This intolerance would have prevented people of different cultures and faiths from coming to North America.

5. Letters should include vivid details about the revival, where it was, who spoke, and specific reactions of those attending. Use the following narrative writing rubric to score students' letters:

4	Student writes a multiple-paragraph letter that includes vivid details and descriptions. Spelling and grammar are correct.
3	Student writes a letter that includes details and descriptions. Spelling and grammar may have a few errors.
2	Student writes a one-paragraph letter that includes some details and descriptions. Spelling and grammar have some serious errors.
1	Student writes a letter that is not organized as a paragraph. It has few or no details or descriptions. There are many serious errors.

Link to ∞ Visual Arts Students' fliers should reflect a description of the emotions that preachers expressed and inspired in those attending.

Intervention

Reading Skill Mini-Lesson   ELA 5RC2.3

Go back into the text and reread the first paragraph on p. 83. The first sentence states the main idea of the paragraph. Ask students to look for three details that will support the main idea.

Analysis Skill Mini-Lesson   HI 3

Help students interpret the cause-and-effect relationship between the First Great Awakening and increased tolerance. Then remind students of the growing intolerance there had been among some religious groups that contradicted the reason many settlers came to America.

Writing Skill Mini-Lesson   ELA 5WA2.1

Tell students that a good narrative contains vivid descriptions of people and the setting.

Ask students to consider how they would feel if they had been living in one of the colonies and attended a revival for the first time. Ask: *Would you be swayed by the preacher's words, or not?* In their letters, they need to capture the spirit of the preacher and the reactions of the public.

Visual Arts Support   VAPA VA2.7

Have students review the images of revivals in this lesson in order to understand the strong emotions from both preachers and audience.

What systems developed in the colonies?

🐻 **California Objective H-SS 5.4.5** Understand how the British colonial period created the basis for the development of political self-government and a free-market economic system and the differences between the British, Spanish, and French colonial systems.

STANDARDS TRACE	
Introduce	Reinforce
pp. **85**T4, **85–88**	pp. **88**T1–T5

Content Paths

✓ Core Instruction	Alternate Instruction	
Text Path, p. **85**T4 Student Text, pp. **85–88** Citizenship: Rules of Civility	**Digital Path**, p. **88**T1 Video: *Colonial Systems*	✋ **Active Path**, pp. **88**T2–T4 *Colonial Williamsburg* Activity: Situation Cards

Big Ideas

Students Will Learn

Teacher Background

In the 1500s and 1600s, French colonists were fur traders, and Spanish colonists had farms or ranches.

New France grew slowly because its economy focused on the fur trade rather than on agriculture, which was the foundation of Spanish and English settlements. In the early 1600s, the French fur trade monopoly ended, the war with the Iroquois hindered the expansion of New France, and war with the English threatened the loss of French control of the colony. Montreal was founded in 1642 as the first of many French mission posts built in the Huron region. Spanish missions also led to the rise of prosperous colonies, and eventually to the *hacienda* system of land estates in North America.

Common Misconception: Students may think that the Spanish empire only included southwestern North America. Let students know that it included present-day Florida and other areas in North America.

English colonists were farmers or townspeople with jobs.

In some families, boys left school as young as eight years old to begin apprenticeships. In Europe apprenticeships were used to train members of guilds, or labor unions. The goal of an apprenticeship was that by age twenty-one, the apprentice mastered a craft and opened his own shop where he would employ his own apprentices.

Different economic systems developed in different regions.

Plantations in the Southern Colonies were mainly owned by Protestant settlers from the British Isles who brought over enslaved Africans and West Indians to provide labor. The main crop in Virginia and North Carolina was tobacco. In the islands off the coast of Georgia and South Carolina, rice and indigo were grown. Mass production of cotton began throughout the South after the invention of the cotton gin by Eli Whitney in 1794. Soon cotton became a staple of the South's agricultural economy.

Government systems developed in the colonies.

The Townshend Revenue Act of 1767 stated specific British imports that would be taxed in the colonies: lead, paint, glass, paper, and tea. Although it was written to help the colonies, many colonists opposed it. John Dickinson of Pennsylvania was a spokesman for colonial rights of self-government.

Reading Transparency R18

Compare and Contrast Use the transparency to recognize comparisons and contrasts. Have students identify comparisons *(both had large amounts of land; fewer settlers than the English colonies)* and contrasts. *(New Spain colonists owned plantations, raised animals and crops, and practiced slavery).*

Related Words Understanding how words are related helps readers learn new terms. An *apprentice* learns a skilled trade, such as iron work or wood carving.

Audio Student Text

(digital) 🔊 A digital audio version of the Student Text is available for students needing auditory support.

Introduce Lesson Vocabulary

For definitions, see p. 85. Look at the words and definitions together. Have students identify how the terms are related. (Apprentices *learn a trade from* artisans. Artisans *create goods or services to sell in a* free-market economy.)

artisan	**town common**
apprentice	**free-market economy**

Assessment

(digital) Lesson Pretest

• Ongoing Assessment pp. **85** T4, **88** T1, **88** T2

• Lesson Assessment p. **88** T6

(digital) Lesson Quiz

Universal Access

English Learners
Colonial Life Help students understand the difficulties of colonial life.

Beginning (Level 1): Using the small map on p. 86, have students compare the size of European territories in North America. Then have them list the countries in order, depending on the size of their territories, from greatest to smallest.

Intermediate (Levels 2–3): Using the image on p. 85, have students create a word web with "changes for colonists" in the center and words or phrases describing these changes in the surrounding bubbles.

Advanced (Levels 4–5): As a group, have students create their own "Rules of Civility" that would have helped colonists get along better with one another.

(digital) 🔊 Audio Student Text

Extra Support
Compare and Contrast Have students use a three-column chart to compare and contrast the economic systems of the Spanish, French, and English colonies. Encourage them to use some of the vocabulary words in their statements.

Identify Main Ideas Have students identify main ideas and supporting details from each section in the lesson to summarize how the economic systems of the Spanish, French, and English colonies developed.

(digital) 🔊 Audio Student Text

Inclusion/Special Needs
Classify Help students put each of the following words or phrases in columns labeled "Spanish," "French," and "English" to indicate which colony(ies) each is associated with: Huron; fur trade; trading posts; plantations; hot and dry climate; ranchers; grasslands; enslaved American Indians and Africans; small family farms; self-sufficient families; artisans.

Access Prior Knowledge Ask students if they have ever moved to a new place. Encourage them to share what new things they had to learn, how they learned those things, and how they made new friends. Relate their responses to the colonists' experiences living in a new place.

(digital) 🔊 Audio Student Text

Challenge
Extend Conversation Lead a discussion about a free-market economy. Discuss how it works and why it was important to colonists not to have prices controlled by the English government. Discuss how prices are determined in this type of system and why it was beneficial to the colonists.

Compare and Contrast Have students discuss the ways in which the economic systems established by the colonists in the 1500s and 1600s were similar to and different from the economic systems in those regions today.

Path Prep

LESSON 5 What systems developed in the colonies?

🐻 H-SS 5.4.5

Pacing	Materials	Assessment
35 MINUTES	• Student Text, pp. **85–88** • Student Text Transparencies, pp. **85–88** • *Find Out More* Handout, p. **88** T5	• **digital** Lesson Pretest • Lesson Assessment, p. **88** T6 • **digital** Lesson Quiz

1 Build Background

Activate Prior Knowledge Ask students what rules they have in their families or classroom. Are there similarities and differences among different sets of rules? Similar to families, England, Spain, and France developed different systems of government and economics for their colonies.

Preview the Lesson Read *Set the Scene* with the class. Draw students' attention to the picture on p. 85. Have volunteers describe the work that is going on, and the feelings people seem to be having.

Introduce Vocabulary After students complete the vocabulary activity on p. 85, discuss what *trades* are, using present-day examples.

2 Teach

Read Together (pp. **86–87**) Remind students that the standard points out the need to understand the differences between English, Spanish, and French colonial systems. Discuss these differences after reading the first section.

Reading Informational Text Use the images from the lesson to discuss what life was like in colonial times. Discuss what in the images makes it appear that life was easier or more difficult then as compared to today.

digital ◀)) **Audio Student Text**

Summarize Before students answer the Lesson Summary on p. 87, suggest that they might want to organize the information in a chart that lists the different ways of life among the Spanish, French, and English colonies.

Citizenship: Rules of Civility REPV 2 (p. **88**) Read the page together. Discuss what similarities and differences these rules have with rules we have today.

Ongoing Assessment ★

▶ **IF** students have difficulty contrasting the way Spanish and French colonists interacted with American Indians (Question 1),

▶ **THEN** remind them that both countries were interested in exploiting the continent's natural resources. The French made money from furs while the Spanish made money by growing crops. The French needed American Indians to obtain the furs. The Spanish needed American Indians for manual labor to grow and harvest crops.

3 Assess and Extend

Lesson Assessment (p. **88** T6)

Extend Go to the Colonial Williamsburg Web site (www.cwf.org) to view the full list of Washington's 110 rules of civility. Have students choose rules to rewrite in modern-day English.

Find Out More (p. **88** T5) After reviewing the page with students, discuss the following questions: *Is such a trade still important today? Which trades still exist today?*

LESSON 5
Overview

LESSON 5
Text Path

LESSON 5
Digital Path

LESSON 5
Active Path

LESSON 5
Assessment

Name:

🐻 **H-SS 5.4.5** Understand how the British colonial period created the basis for the development of political self-government and a free-market economic system and the differences between the British, Spanish, and French colonial systems.

Unit 4 • Life in the Colonies
Lesson 5

What systems developed in the colonies?

SET THE SCENE Suppose you moved to a new town or city. You would have to figure out new ways of doing things, such as getting to school. In the 1500s, colonists from Spain, France, and England began arriving in North America. How did life change for them once they arrived?

Preview the Lesson
Vocabulary

artisan *(n.)* a skilled worker who makes things by hand

apprentice *(n.)* a person who learns a skill or trade from an experienced worker

town common *(n.)* an open space in the center of a town where cattle and sheep could graze

free-market economy *(n.)* a system in which prices are not controlled by the government

Vocabulary Activity Draw an arrow to connect the two vocabulary words above that describe people who might work together. Which one would learn from the other? Circle that word.

Reading: Compare and Contrast

Comparing and contrasting ideas can help you see how ideas are related. As you read the first paragraph on page 86, underline details about New Spain and New France that you could compare in order to better understand how people in both colonies worked with American Indians.

85

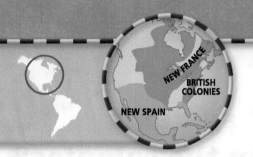

Spanish and French Colonies

In the 1500s and 1600s, France and Spain began to found and settle colonies in North America. As you have learned, the French developed trade relationships with several American Indian groups. The fur trade brought huge profits to the French, who built trading posts throughout New France. Settlements in New Spain, however, focused on agriculture. Plantations were an important part of the Spanish colonies, but the hot, dry climate in some areas of New Spain did not allow crop farming. In areas with grasslands, sheep and cattle ranches were developed instead. On both plantations and ranches, much of the work was done by enslaved American Indians and Africans.

Life in the English Colonies

The English colonies attracted more people than the French and Spanish colonies did. These colonists came for many different reasons but worked hard once they got here. In the New England and Middle Colonies, most people lived in small towns or on family farms. All family members, including children, worked together to make or grow what the family needed.

Soon, other work roles developed. **Artisans** were skilled workers who made things by hand. They made goods such as barrels for storage and iron goods, such as nails and horseshoes. Artisans often hired apprentices to help them. An **apprentice** is a person who learns a skill or trade from an experienced worker.

1. **Compare the ways in which Spanish and French colonists interacted with American Indians.**
Compare and Contrast

French colonists traded furs with American Indians, while Spanish colonists forced enslaved American Indians and Africans to work on plantations and ranches.

2. **How did family farms become self-sufficient?** *Cause and Effect*

All family members worked together to make or grow most of what the family needed.

Tools, brought mostly from England, allowed artisans to practice trades such as carpentry.

86 • Life in the Colonies

Economic Systems Develop

Different kinds of settlements and economic systems formed in the English colonial regions. In the Southern Colonies, wealthy farmers ran large plantations that depended on enslaved people to work in the fields. The crops they grew were shipped to other colonies and to England.

Small towns developed throughout New England and the Middle Colonies. Many New England towns had a **town common,** which was an open space in the center of a town where cattle and sheep could graze. Families also owned small plots of land for farming. Towns in the Middle Colonies often served as busy trading centers, where farmers from the area came to sell their crops and buy items like clothing and tools. Meeting needs through trade allowed free-market economies to develop in these towns. In a **free-market economy,** prices are not controlled by the government.

Cities developed throughout the colonies and served as major trading centers. From coastal cities, merchants exported goods such as flour and wheat. They also imported goods the colonies did not produce, such as sugar and spices, as well as manufactured goods, such as tools and cloth.

Government Systems Develop

For the most part, the colonies governed themselves and acted independently of England. Colonial governments handled most of the everyday decisions. However, England did set laws on how goods could be traded to and from the colonies. These laws sometimes went against the idea of a free-market economy. This issue would later lead to conflicts between the colonists and England.

Summary Answer Trade influenced life in new France, while life in New Spain was influenced by agriculture. Ways of life in the English colonies varied in different regions, based on a combination of trade and agriculture.

3. What role did cities play in all three colonial regions? *Compare and Contrast*

They served as major trading centers.

The economy of the Southern Colonies focused on exporting tobacco and other cash crops.

4. Underline a sentence that tells one way England governed the colonies. *Main Idea and Details*

Summary

France, Spain, and England each developed different systems for their North American colonies. Summarize how different ways of life developed in the French, Spanish, and English colonies.

Unit 4 Lesson 5 • **87**

Citizenship

Rules of Civility

Learn More Education was an important part of life in the colonies. There were few formal schools, but people learned in different ways. Apprentices learned skills from artisans. In 1636 Puritans founded Harvard College in Cambridge, Massachusetts. In 1642 Massachusetts passed a law that required parents to teach their children to read.

Much of the reading students did was about religion and good manners. While still a young student, a Virginia colonist named George Washington copied 110 "rules of civility," or polite behavior, into his notebook. These rules helped teach young people proper behavior so that they would become good citizens and valuable members of society. Many of the rules are still useful today.

Read the rules of civility listed to the right. Then answer these questions.

1. Circle the numbers of two rules that would be most useful to remember when you are in a quiet place, such as a library. *Interpret*

2. Which of these rules do you think is most important? Rewrite it in your own words. *Apply*

Answers will vary.

_____

_____

_____

_____

_____

_____

_____

Rule 1: Every Action done in Company, ought to be with Some Sign of Respect, to those that are Present.

Rule 4: In the Presence of Others Sing not to yourself with a humming Noise, nor Drum with your Fingers or Feet.

Rule 5: If You Cough, Sneeze, Sigh, or Yawn, do it not Loud but Privately; and Speak not in your Yawning, but put Your handkercheif or Hand before your face and turn aside.

Rule 6: Sleep not when others Speak, Sit not when others stand, Speak not when you Should hold your Peace, walk not on when others Stop.

88 • **Life in the Colonies**

Digital Path

LESSON 5 **What systems developed in the colonies?**

H-SS 5.4.5

Path Prep	Pacing	Materials	Assessment
	50 MINUTES	· Video: *Colonial Systems* · Interactive Practice: *The Birth of New Systems* · Print Partner: *New Systems Emerge* · **digital** 🔊 Audio Student Text	· **digital** Lesson Pretest · Lesson Assessment, p. **88**T6 · **digital** Lesson Quiz

1 Build Background

Activate Prior Knowledge Have students think about the groups and organizations in their community that serve the people, such as the schools, the police force, and the local government. Ask: *Why do you think that these kinds of things are important to a community?*

Introduce Vocabulary Introduce the lesson vocabulary words using the print or digital cards.

Lesson Introduction Launch the Lesson Introduction, which asks the question, "What systems developed in the colonies?"

2 Teach

Video As students view *Colonial Systems,* have them consider these questions:
• What systems developed in the colonies?
• Why did they arise?
• Who benefited from the changes? Who did not?

Interactive Practice Launch the activity, *The Birth of New Systems.* The activity will help students understand that the different systems that developed in the colonies were born out of necessity.

Print Partner In this activity, students will complete a chart related to the economic

systems and government that developed in the colonies.

digital 🔊 **Audio Student Text**

Ongoing *Assessment* ★

▶ **IF** students are struggling to understand what a free-market economy is,

▶ **THEN** draw the graphic below on the board. Review the information with students to explain the interplay of supply and demand that occurs in a free-market economy.
• many goods = less demand = lower prices
• fewer goods = greater demand = higher prices

3 Assess and Extend

digital **Lesson Quiz** Have students check their understanding of the lesson content by answering the questions. After students complete the page, review the answers with the class.

Lesson Assessment Use the assessment on p. **88**T6 to evaluate students' comprehension of the lesson.

Extend Have students form small groups and assign each group a French, Spanish, or English colonial colony in North America to research. Instruct each group to explore what life was like in the assigned colony. Tell students to find out the kinds of jobs people held in the colony, how the people were governed, and what kind of economy developed. Have each group present their report to the class. Students can then discuss which colony they would choose to live in and tell why.

Active Path

Colonial Williamsburg

LESSON 5 **What systems developed in the colonies?**

🐻 H-SS 5.4.5

Description: Students will explore the colonial system in a simulation activity.

Path Prep

Pacing	Materials	Assessment
50 MINUTES	· Sixty 3 x 5 index cards · Ten 9 x 12 sheets of construction paper · Handouts, pp. **88**T3–T4	· **digital** Lesson Pretest · Lesson Assessment, p. **88**T6 · **digital** Lesson Quiz

1 Build Background

Activate Prior Knowledge Discuss the different ways European countries colonized North America. The Spanish enslaved natives, mined precious metals, and established missions to convert native peoples to Catholicism. The French built fur trading posts and traded with native peoples. French Jesuits lived among American Indians to convert them to Catholicism. The English built communities that shipped raw materials to England in trade for manufactured goods.

Introduce Vocabulary Go over the lesson vocabulary words on p. 85.

2 Teach

Introduce Activity Explain to students that they will role play to understand the English colonial system.

Activity Steps

1. Divide the class into ten groups. Give each group one card from the *Situation Cards* handouts, six index cards and a piece of construction paper.

2. Explain that each group represents the person on their card. Have each group write its identity on the six index cards and use the construction paper to design a sign identifying the group.

3. Explain that you (the teacher) represent English Parliament and the king. Because Parliament and the king have protected them, everyone must pay a tax. Collect two cards from each group.

4. Explain to students that the remaining cards represent goods and services to be traded. Have the groups follow the directions on their situation card and transact the business as indicated.

5. Have students count their cards. They should see that the English merchants, Parliament, and the king have the most cards. Ask: *Who benefited from the English colonial system?*

Ongoing *Assessment* ★

▶ **IF** students have problems understanding how trade between the colonies and mother country worked,

▶ **THEN** remind students that the colonies produced raw materials and the mother country manufactured products from those raw materials. The manufactured products were then sold to the colonies.

3 Assess and Extend

Assess Have students write a paragraph for a colonial American newspaper that describes the English colonial system. Is it fair or unfair? Why or why not?

Lesson Assessment (p. **88**T6)

Extend Have each group research their trade or occupation and give a presentation for the class explaining the kinds of products that their occupation made or traded.

Situation Cards 1

Small Farmer

You are a small farmer living in colonial America. You grow some wheat and raise a few cattle.

1. Sell your crop of wheat to the local storekeeper. The storekeeper should give you two cards.
2. Buy a pair of shoes from the shoemaker. Give the shoemaker one card.
3. Buy a newspaper from the printer. Give the printer one card.
4. Have the miller grind your corn into flour. Give the miller one card.

Plantation Owner

You are a large plantation owner in colonial America and own many enslaved people. You grow tobacco.

1. Sell your crop of tobacco to the English merchant. The English merchant should give you two cards.
2. Buy barrels in which to pack your tobacco. Pay the cooper one card.
3. Buy a new dining room table from the English merchant. Pay the English merchant one card.
4. Pay the miller to grind your corn into flour. Pay the miller one card.

Storekeeper

You are a small storekeeper in colonial America.

1. Buy supplies from the English merchant. Give the English merchant two cards.
2. Place an advertisement in the newspaper. Pay the printer one card.
3. Pay the cooper one card to make barrels for you.

Carpenter

You are a carpenter living in colonial America. You build and repair buildings.

1. Buy nails from the storekeeper. Pay the storekeeper one card.
2. Buy medicine from the apothecary. Pay the apothecary one card.
3. Buy a pair of shoes from the shoemaker. Pay the shoemaker one card.

Situation Cards 2

Cooper

You are a cooper living in colonial America. You make barrels for shipping things.

1. Buy tools from the storekeeper. Pay the storekeeper one card.
2. Pay the printer to place an advertisement in the newspaper. Pay the printer one card.
3. Buy medicine from the apothecary. Pay the apothecary one card.

English Merchant

You are a merchant who lives in London. You buy tobacco from colonial America and sell manufactured goods to Americans.

Apothecary

You are an apothecary living in colonial America. You make medicine for people.

1. Buy medicine from the English merchant. Pay the English merchant two cards.
2. Pay the printer to put an advertisement in the newspaper. Pay the printer one card.
3. Pay the carpenter to repair the door of your shop. Pay the carpenter one card.

Miller

You are a miller living in colonial America. You grind wheat into flour and corn into meal.

1. Buy supplies from the storekeeper. Pay the storekeeper one card.
2. Buy medicine from the apothecary. Pay the apothecary one card.
3. Pay the carpenter to fix your mill. Pay the carpenter one card.

Printer

You are a printer living in colonial America. You publish a newspaper once a week.

1. Buy paper and ink from the English merchant. Pay the English merchant two cards.
2. Buy a pair of shoes from the shoemaker. Pay the shoemaker one card.
3. Pay the carpenter to fix your window. Pay the carpenter one card.

Shoemaker

You are a shoemaker living in colonial America. You make shoes.

1. Buy leather from the English merchant. Pay the English merchant two cards.
2. Buy supplies from the storekeeper. Pay the storekeeper one card.
3. Buy medicine from the apothecary. Pay the apothecary one card.

Name: _____

Unit 4 Lesson 5

Colonial Jobs

As you have learned, most colonists lived on farms. As the colonies grew, however, there was a wider variety of ways that people could make a living. The chart below shows some of the different types of jobs the colonists had.

Job	What They Did
 Shoemaker	Made shoes from leather and wood
 Blacksmith	Made and repaired iron goods, such as horseshoes, axes, gun parts, and nails
 Fisherman	Caught fish in the Atlantic Ocean
 Cooper	Made barrels from wood and iron
 Printer	Printed posters, newspapers, and books
 Surveyor	Made maps and marked boundary lines
 Miller	Ran mills where colonists could grind corn and wheat into flour
 Merchant	Traded goods with England and other countries
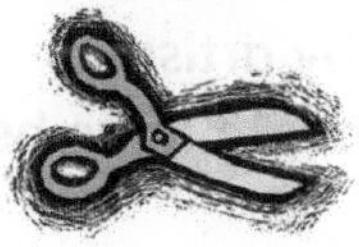 Dressmaker	Made clothes from woven material

Name: _____

What systems developed in the colonies?

1. Compare and Contrast: Compare and contrast the English, French, and Spanish colonial systems in the chart below.

English, French, and Spanish Colonial Systems

Alike	Different

2. *Recall* List the types of items that an **artisan** might have produced.

_____

_____

3. *Analyze* How did the growth of cities and towns in the colonies lead to the development of a **free-market economy**?

_____

_____

4. *Evaluate* England set laws on trade to and from the colonies. Why do you think this might lead to conflicts between colonists and England? Explain your answer.

_____

_____

5. **Write a Narrative** You are a colonial farmer living in the Middle Colonies. Write a point-of-view narrative about the economic system in your area, describing the crops you grow to sell in the town and the items you buy there.

Link to ∞ Economics Make a chart that lists colonial products made by artisans. Assign prices for each item based on what you think the value of each item might have been.

Lesson 5 Assessment

Answers

1.

English, French, and Spanish Colonial Systems

English and Spanish developed agriculture and had enslaved people.	French developed trade with American Indians and developed the fur trade. The English had more settlers and small farms.
Alike	**Different**

2. Nails, horseshoes, barrels, iron goods

3. Towns and cities were also trading centers. Farmers came to towns to sell and buy products. Colonists exported and imported goods from cities. This trading allowed free-market societies to develop.

4. Possible answer: English laws on trade may lead to conflict because this went against the idea of a free-market society and the colonists would not want England to be involved.

5. Students' narratives should contain details about the farm, the farmer's daily routine, and how the farmer trades products in the town common. Use the following narrative writing rubric to score students' work:

4	Student writes a multiple-paragraph narrative that includes realistic details. Spelling and grammar are correct.
3	Student writes one or two paragraphs that include some details. Spelling and grammar may have a few errors.
2	Student writes a one-paragraph narrative that includes few details. Spelling and grammar have some serious errors.
1	Narrative is not organized as a paragraph. It has few or no details. There are many serious errors.

Link to ⚯ Economics Students should include products that were discussed in the lesson. Prices will vary.

Intervention

Reading Skill Mini-Lesson   **ELA 5RC2.1**

Reread "Spanish and French Colonies" on p. 86. Ask students to look for information that compares and contrasts these colonial systems. Have students look for compare and contrast signal words such as *both*.

Analysis Skill Mini-Lesson   **HI 3**

To help students understand how this could cause conflict, remind them that the colonists enjoyed some self-government and independence from England. English laws on trade would affect America's emerging free-market society and force the colonists to live with prices the English government imposed on goods.

Writing Skill Mini-Lesson   **ELA 5WA2.1**

Tell students that a good narrative contains believable details.

Brainstorm with students the different crops or animals that a farmer might have raised in colonial New England and ask students to choose one or several of these for the farm. Review the purpose of a town common.

Economics Support   **H-SS 5.4.5**

Direct students to encyclopedias or *.edu* Web sites that provide details about products made in colonial America.

What was the role of slavery in colonial America?

 California Objective H-SS 5.4.6 Describe the introduction of slavery into America, the responses of slave families to their condition, the ongoing struggle between proponents and opponents of slavery, and the gradual institutionalization of slavery in the South.

STANDARDS TRACE	
Introduce	Reinforce
pp. **89**T4, **89–92**	pp. **92**T1–T5, **149–152**

✔ Core Instruction	Alternate Instruction	
Content Paths		

Content Paths

✔ **Core Instruction**

📝 **Text Path, p. 89**T4
Student Text, pp. **89–92**
Primary Source: Autobiographies

Alternate Instruction

📱 **Digital Path, p. 92**T1
Video: *Slavery in Colonial America*

✋ **Active Path, p. 92**T2–T4
Colonial Williamsburg
Activity: Analyzing Primary Sources

Big Ideas

Students Will Learn

American Indians and later Africans were enslaved to work in the Americas.

Enslaved Africans faced many hardships.

Many people resisted slavery.

Teacher Background

On Spanish missions, enslaved American Indians made up most of the labor force. In California approximately sixty percent of mortalities among American Indians on missions was due to diseases brought over by Europeans. Spanish settlers used African slave labor in settlements along the Atlantic Coast, and in the Caribbean, such as Puerto Rico. Portuguese settlers brought enslaved Africans to work on plantations in Brazil. By 1619 enslaved Africans began to arrive in Virginia.

Common Misconception: Students may not know that slavery had existed in other places and other times than the Americas, and it was not only Africans who had been enslaved. Explain that slavery has existed in many places, including South and Central America, in Africa itself, as well as the Middle East and ancient Greece and Rome. Conditions of slavery often differed. In some societies, slaves were persons accused of crimes. American Indians took captives as slaves, but they were often integrated into the tribe, and their enslaved status was not lasting.

Benin is a country located in West Africa, along the Atlantic Coast near Ghana. It was part of a powerful kingdom named Dahomey at the time that the European slave trade began. African kingdoms had been at war, and some groups moved to the coast to have access to firearms and other European goods that arrived in the ports. In 1807 Britain declared the slave trade illegal and ordered British merchants to cease. This reduced the trade but did not stop it.

Starting in the 1500s, every slave society in the Americas experienced revolts. In 1739 despite formal restrictions on their rights, some enslaved Africans in South Carolina were growing their own food, assembling in groups, earning money, and learning to read. However, after a bloody rebellion at Stono River, the South Carolina government placed severe limits on enslaved people's rights. Nat Turner led a deadly but unsuccessful revolt in Southampton, Virginia, in 1831. One of the most significant rebellions in the Americas was led by Toussaint-Louverture, a formerly enslaved African, in the French colony of St. Domingue in 1791. Even though France had freed all their enslaved people by 1794, the Africans continued to fight for independence from France, creating a new country, Haiti, in 1804.

Reading Transparency R19

 Make Generalizations Use the transparency before teaching the lesson to make the generalization that *the need for workers (labor) led to the increase of slavery.*

Synonyms/Antonyms Recall that antonyms are opposite words and synonyms are similar words. Read the sentence and ask students to determine that *opponent* is an antonym.

Audio Student Text

`digital` ◀)) A digital audio version of the Student Text is available for students needing auditory support.

Introduce Lesson Vocabulary

For definitions, see p. 89. Discuss the words and definitions together. Ask students to determine the correct words: The slaves will *(rebel)* against the *(proponents)* of the *(auction)* where they were to be sold.

auction	**rebel**
proponent	

`digital` Lesson Pretest

• Ongoing Assessment pp. **89** T4, **92** T1, **92** T2

• Lesson Assessment p. **92** T6

`digital` Lesson Quiz

English Learners

Slavery Help students understand the role of enslaved people in colonial America.

Beginning (Level 1): Ask students to help you create a list of ways in which enslaved people tried to gain their freedom: escape, buying their freedom, seeking to abolish slavery, and asking their owners to free them.

Intermediate (Levels 2–3): Using the information in the lesson, create a chart of the hardships imposed on enslaved people.

Advanced (Levels 4–5): Have students identify the views of *proponents* and opponents of slavery.

 `digital` ◀)) Audio Student Text

Extra Support

Summarize Have students write the main idea and supporting details from each section in the lesson to summarize the role of slavery in colonial America.

Make Generalizations Ask students to use each of the following words in a sentence to make generalizations about slavery in colonial America: *plantations; auction; rebel; Africans; freedom.*

`digital` ◀)) Audio Student Text

Inclusion/Special Needs

Model Concepts Review the definition of the word *auction*, then hold an auction with students. Write the names of items to be auctioned off on cards and model for students how an auction is conducted.

Compare and Contrast Lead a discussion about what it must have been like to be an enslaved person in colonial America. Ask students to consider how their lives would be different if they were slaves. Make a two-column chart with column headings "Life of Freedom" and "Life of Slavery." Write students' responses in the chart as you discuss slavery.

 `digital` ◀)) Audio Student Text

Challenge

Predict Lead a discussion about the impact of slavery on the economy of the Southern Colonies. Ask students how the economy of the colonies would have been different had the plantation owners not had access to free labor to run their plantations. Discuss the advantage the Southern Colonies had in a free-market economic system over the colonies that did not use slave labor.

Use a Primary Source Have students find a primary source to learn more about what it was like for enslaved people in colonial America. Ask them to describe the source they used, tell where they found it, and summarize its content.

LESSON 6 What was the role of slavery in colonial North America?

🐻 H-SS 5.4.6

Path Prep

Pacing

35 MINUTES

Materials
- Student Text, pp. **89–92**
- Student Text Transparencies, pp. **89–92**
- *Find Out More* Handout, p. **92**T5

Assessment
- digital Lesson Pretest
- Lesson Assessment, p. **92**T6
- digital Lesson Quiz

1 Build Background

Activate Prior Knowledge Invite students to create lists of jobs or chores they do at school or home. Have students discuss if they would do these jobs if they were forced to do them without getting paid.

Preview the Lesson Read *Set the Scene* with the class. Discuss the image of a slave auction on p. 89. Plantations needed many people to work the fields to produce cash crops. More and more

plantation owners relied on enslaved Africans to get the work done cheaply. Explain to students that they will find out about the hardships faced by enslaved people.

Introduce Vocabulary After students complete the vocabulary activity on p. 89, ask them to review the definition for the verb *rebel*. What do they think the noun form of the word means?

2 Teach

Read Together (pp. **90–91**) Explain the term *institutionalization* from the standard. After each section, pause to discuss what factors led to the institutionalization of slavery in the colonies.

Reading Informational Text Using the image on p. 90, have students make a list of words that describe conditions on slave ships from Africa to the Americas, often called the "Middle Passage."

digital ◄)) **Audio Student Text**

Summarize As students write their answers to the Lesson Summary on p. 91, remind them to include slavery's effect on both enslaved people and colonists.

Find Out More HI 1 (p. **92**T5) Have students read the page and then write a few

sentences describing Sewall's reasons for opposing slavery and then discuss with the class.

Primary Source: Autobiographies REPV 2 (p.**92**) Explain to students that most enslaved people were not allowed to learn to read and write. Have students discuss why owners of enslaved people would enforce such rules.

Ongoing *Assessment* ★

▶ **IF** students have trouble finding details to support the generalization (Question 1),

▶ **THEN** remind them that a main goal of the colonists was to make money by exploiting North America's natural resources. To do this, colonists needed workers. Guide students to look for how Spanish and English colonists met these labor needs.

3 Assess and Extend

Lesson Assessment (p. **92**T6)

Extend Have students research the role of spirituals in the everyday life of enslaved Africans.

Name:

H-SS 5.4.6 Describe the introduction of slavery into America, the responses of slave families to their condition, the ongoing struggle between proponents and opponents of slavery, and the gradual institutionalization of slavery in the South.

Lesson 6

What was the role of slavery in colonial America?

Preview the Lesson
Vocabulary

auction *(n.)* a public sale in which something is sold to the person who offers the most money

proponent *(n.)* a person who supports something

rebel *(v.)* to resist or fight against authority

Vocabulary Activity *Opponents* are people who fight or speak against something. Circle the vocabulary word above that is an antonym for *opponent.*

People
Olaudah Equiano

SET THE SCENE When we do work, we usually receive something in return for our effort. As you have learned, American colonists needed many people to help do their work. However, enslaved people lived lives of hardship and received no pay in return.

⊙ Reading: Make Generalizations

A *generalization* is a broad statement about people or places that is true most of the time. As you read the second paragraph on page 90, underline a sentence that makes a generalization about slavery in the Southern Colonies.

89

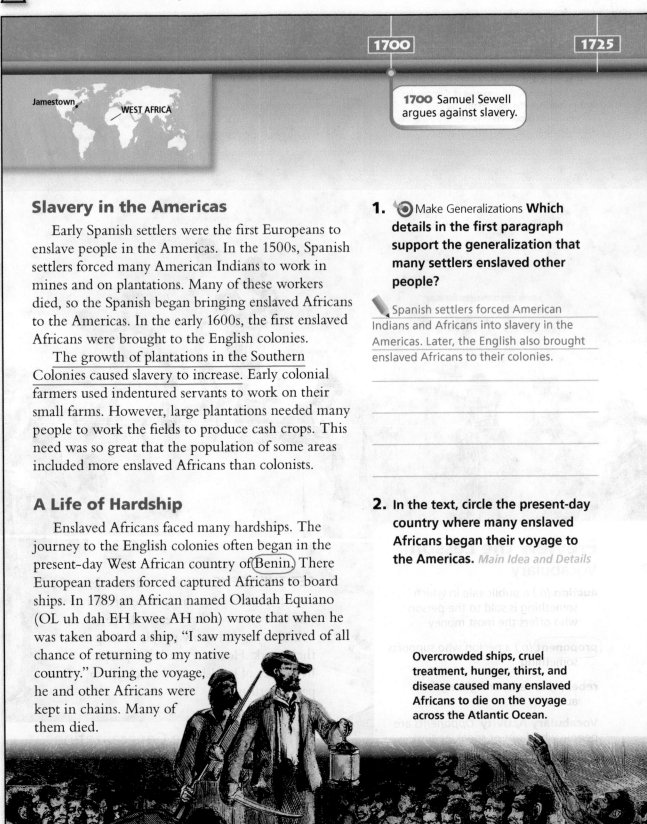

| | 1700 | 1725 |

Jamestown, WEST AFRICA

1700 Samuel Sewell argues against slavery.

Slavery in the Americas

Early Spanish settlers were the first Europeans to enslave people in the Americas. In the 1500s, Spanish settlers forced many American Indians to work in mines and on plantations. Many of these workers died, so the Spanish began bringing enslaved Africans to the Americas. In the early 1600s, the first enslaved Africans were brought to the English colonies.

The growth of plantations in the Southern Colonies caused slavery to increase. Early colonial farmers used indentured servants to work on their small farms. However, large plantations needed many people to work the fields to produce cash crops. This need was so great that the population of some areas included more enslaved Africans than colonists.

A Life of Hardship

Enslaved Africans faced many hardships. The journey to the English colonies often began in the present-day West African country of Benin. There European traders forced captured Africans to board ships. In 1789 an African named Olaudah Equiano (OL uh dah EH kwee AH noh) wrote that when he was taken aboard a ship, "I saw myself deprived of all chance of returning to my native country." During the voyage, he and other Africans were kept in chains. Many of them died.

1. Make Generalizations **Which details in the first paragraph support the generalization that many settlers enslaved other people?**

Spanish settlers forced American Indians and Africans into slavery in the Americas. Later, the English also brought enslaved Africans to their colonies.

2. **In the text, circle the present-day country where many enslaved Africans began their voyage to the Americas.** *Main Idea and Details*

Overcrowded ships, cruel treatment, hunger, thirst, and disease caused many enslaved Africans to die on the voyage across the Atlantic Ocean.

| 1750 | 1775 | 1800 |

1739 Enslaved Africans revolt in Stono Rebellion.

1789 Olaudah Equiano writes about his life as an enslaved African.

The hardships of enslaved Africans continued when the ship reached the colonies. Traders sold them as property at auctions. An **auction** is a public sale in which something is sold to the person who offers the most money. Sometimes family members were sold to different owners. After they were purchased, most enslaved people worked in plantation fields. They often worked many hours under the hot sun. Others worked in the owner's house. They cooked and took care of the family's children. Whatever they did, enslaved people faced punishment if they disobeyed their owner. In most cases, they were enslaved for life.

Resistance to Slavery

Many colonists and enslaved people resisted slavery. In 1700 colonist Samuel Sewall wrote, "[A]ll Men . . . have equal Rights unto Liberty." Many Quakers also opposed slavery. However, other colonists were proponents of slavery. **Proponents** are people who support something. In the South, many colonists supported slavery and encouraged its spread.

Enslaved people often rebelled against their owners in many ways. To **rebel** is to resist or fight against authority. Some people rebelled by working slowly or running away. Others, such as Equiano, saved money and bought their freedom. Sometimes they even rebelled by fighting. The Stono Rebellion took place in South Carolina in 1739. In this rebellion, about 100 enslaved people tried to escape but were later recaptured. Even those people who did not openly rebel resisted slavery by keeping their African culture alive through music, dance, and stories.

Summary Answer Slavery made large plantations possible, but it led to hardships for enslaved people. They and others resisted slavery, but many others supported and encouraged its spread.

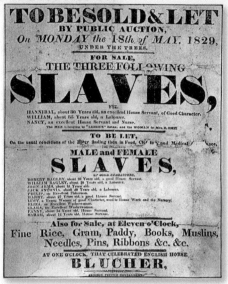

Auctions for enslaved people were announced by posters such as this.

3. Underline ways in which enslaved people resisted their owners.

Main Idea and Details

Summary

The growth of colonial plantations led to the use of enslaved people as workers. How did slavery affect life in the American colonies?

Unit 4 Lesson 6 • **91**

LESSON 6 Overview

LESSON 6 Text Path

LESSON 6 Digital Path

LESSON 6 Active Path

LESSON 6 Assessment

Autobiographies: Olaudah Equiano

Learn More An autobiography is a primary source in which a person tells his or her life story. Olaudah Equiano was born in the West African country of Nigeria. At the age of eleven, he was kidnapped, sold into slavery, and shipped to Barbados. Over time he was sold again and again to owners in Virginia and Philadelphia. Equiano was twenty-one years old before he was able to buy his freedom. He moved to Britain and wrote the first autobiography by a freed enslaved African, *The Interesting Narrative of the Life of Olaudah Equiano, or Gustavus Vassa, the African*, which was published in 1789. Read the passage from Equiano's autobiography and then answer the questions.

1. In the passage, circle the name that Equiano had chosen for himself. *Identify*

2. Underline the information that explains what happened when Equiano refused to answer to the name Gustavus Vassa. *Identify*

3. Why do you think enslaved people, like Equiano, were not allowed to keep their African names? *Analyze*

Possible answer: It was a way for Europeans to remove Africans from their past and show their new status as property.

_____

_____

_____

"While I was on board this ship, my captain and master named me Gustavus Vassa. I at that time began to understand him a little, and refused to be called so, and told him as well as I could that I would be called Jacob; but he said I should not, and still called me Gustavus: and when I refused to answer to my new name, which I at first did, it gained me many a cuff [hit]; so at length I submitted, and by which I have been known ever since."

92 • Life in the Colonies

Digital Path

LESSON 6 **What was the role of slavery in colonial America?**  H-SS 5.4.6

Path Prep	Pacing ⬤ 50 MINUTES	Materials · Video: *Slavery in Colonial America* · Interactive Practice: *Slavery in the Colonies* · Print Partner: *Africans Face Captivity* · **digital** 🔊 Audio Student Text	Assessment · **digital** Lesson Pretest · Lesson Assessment, p. **92**T6 · **digital** Lesson Quiz

1 Build Background

Activate Prior Knowledge Invite students to share what they know about slavery. Record students' ideas on the board. Add information as students work through the lesson.

Introduce Vocabulary Introduce the lesson vocabulary words using the print or digital cards.

Lesson Introduction Launch the Lesson Introduction, which asks the question, "What was the role of slavery in colonial America?"

2 Teach

Video As students view *Slavery in Colonial America,* have them consider these questions:
• What led to slavery in the Americas?
• What hardships did enslaved Africans endure?
• How did some people react to slavery?

Interactive Practice Launch the activity, *Slavery in the Colonies.* The activity will help students understand that slavery was the result of people's attitudes as well as economic conditions. Students will also learn that many people in colonial America resisted slavery.

Print Partner Ask students to complete the Print Partner activity. In the activity,

students will answer questions about slavery in the colonies.

digital 🔊 **Audio Student Text**

Ongoing *Assessment* ★

▶ **IF** students are struggling to understand how slavery could have existed in the United States,

▶ **THEN** explain that slavery has existed throughout world history. Share some examples: ancient Egyptians and Romans enslaved people; American Indians of one group would enslave members of other American Indian groups.

3 Assess and Extend

digital **Lesson Quiz** Have students check their understanding of the lesson content by answering the questions. After students complete the page, review the answers with the class.

Lesson Assessment Use the assessment on p. **92**T6 to evaluate students' lesson comprehension.

Extend Distribute copies of the Thirteenth Amendment (slavery outlawed, 1865). Explain the significance of the amendment. Then invite volunteers to read aloud the text as students follow along. Discuss how it is important to continue to protect the freedom of all people even today. Then have students design buttons for an international freedom campaign.

LESSON 6 Overview · LESSON 6 Text Path · LESSON 6 Digital Path · LESSON 6 Active Path · LESSON 6 Assessment

Active Path

Colonial Williamsburg

LESSON 6 What was the role of slavery in colonial North America?   H-SS 5.4.6

Description: Students will complete activities to develop empathy and understanding of the role of slavery in the colonies.

Path Prep	Pacing	Materials	Assessment
	TWO 50-MINUTE SESSIONS	· Handouts, pp. **92** T3–T4	· digital Lesson Pretest · Lesson Assessment, p. **92** T6 · digital Lesson Quiz

1 Build Background

Activate Prior Knowledge Explain that the Portuguese and Spanish were the first European countries to enslave people in Central and South America. Colonial Americans needed a source of labor. Enslaved people filled that need. Explain that prior to the American Revolution every colony, even those in the north, had slavery. Remind students that Africans were brought to colonial America forcibly as part of the "Triangular Trade" (raw materials were shipped to Europe; European trade goods were then shipped to Africa; finally enslaved people were bought in Africa and transported to the Americas). The voyage of enslaved people from Africa to the Americas is known as the "Middle Passage."

Introduce Vocabulary Go over the vocabulary and activity on p. 89. Discuss the terms *proponent* and *opponent*.

2 Teach

Introduce Activity Explain to students that they will be analyzing primary sources from the eighteenth century. These sources depict various aspects of slavery and will help them understand slavery's impact on life in the colonial period.

Activity Steps
1. Organize the class into four groups. Give each student the *Images of Slavery* handouts. Have each group analyze one of the images and answer the questions associated with it.

2. Have a member of each group report the group's findings to the class. As the reports are

presented, the rest of the class should answer the related questions on their *Images of Slavery* handouts.

3. Lead a discussion in which students discuss the points of view of proponents and opponents of slavery.

Ongoing Assessment ★

▶ **IF** students have trouble gathering information from the pictures,

▶ **THEN** have them make a diagram by drawing a line from a part of the picture and write a short description of that part of the image.

3 Assess and Extend

Assess Based on the information they learned in this activity, have each student create a Venn diagram comparing the views of proponents and opponents of slavery.

Lesson Assessment (p. **92** T6)

Extend Have students create an anti-slavery poster. The poster should identify one reason why proponents thought slavery was important and explain why that reason is not valid.

Unit 4 Lesson 6
Images of Slavery 1

Directions: Examine your assigned image and answer the questions associated with it. Be prepared to report your findings to the class.

Engraving: Slave Ship Packing

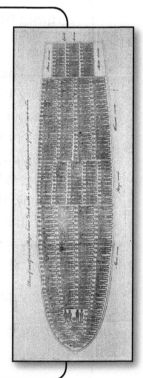

This engraving is titled "Plan of an African Ship's Lower Deck with Negroes." It was printed in Philadelphia, Pennsylvania, in 1797. The diagram shows how tightly enslaved Africans were packed together for the Middle Passage from Africa to North America. As many as half of these enslaved people would die during the voyage (from dysentery or other diseases, poor food and living conditions, or simply from despair). People opposed to the slave trade printed diagrams such as this one to show others the cruel conditions of the slave trade.

1. Estimate (guess) how many people are represented in this picture. Now try to do an exact count. How close was your estimate?

2. Why do you think enslaved people were kept on the lower deck of the ship?

3. How might this picture convince people that slavery was wrong?

Watercolor: "Every Day's Observation..."

This watercolor comes from the sketchbook of Lewis Miller (ca. 1853–1854) in Montgomery County, Virginia. The enslaved people in the foreground are sawing a log to make shingles. You can see the shingle maker working in the background under the tree. The man in the center is probably the overseer. There is also a white laborer on the right side of the picture.

1. What is this probably a scene of?

2. How is each person dressed?

3. What would people who opposed slavery say about what is going on in the picture?

Images of Slavery 2

Directions: Examine your assigned image and answer the questions associated with it. Be prepared to report your findings to the class.

Virginia Gazette Newspaper Advertisement

This advertisement about a runaway enslaved person appeared in the February 15, 1770, *Virginia Gazette* newspaper. The advertisement gives a very complete description of the enslaved person's physical appearance, including the clothes he was wearing when he ran away. The fact that he is thought to be running to his former owner's property suggests he probably had family still living with his old master.

> RUN away from the subscriber, in *Halifax*, on the 13th ult. a negro fellow named CUFFEY, about 25 years old, five feet six inches high, a slender built fellow, very sensible, speaks tolerable good *English*, though *Jamaica* born; he had on when he went away a lightish coloured *Newmarket* coat, a red short jacket, old blue breeches, old felt hat much torn, old shoes, with pewter buckles. He was formerly the property of Mr. *Joseph Williams*, in *Duplin* county, *North Carolina*, on the waters of *Cape Fear*, and it is supposed will endeavour to make his escape that way, with an excuse that he now belongs to Mr. *Williams*, and is going to where he formerly lived. Whoever apprehends the said negro, so that his owner may get him again, shall have 20 s. reward, and if taken in *Carolina* 40 s. besides what the law allows.   2J   JAMES SMITH.

1. Why did the owner put an advertisement in the newspaper?

2. How is Cuffey described?

3. Why is there a reward for Cuffey's return?

Medallion: "Am I Not a Man and a Brother?"

This medallion (a round or oval decoration or medal) was made by Josiah Wedgwood in Staffordshire, England, c. 1787. It was first adopted by the Society for the Abolition of the Slave Trade in England. The picture of an enslaved African in chains kneeling as if pleading for help became the long-lasting emblem of abolitionists and opponents to slavery on both sides of the Atlantic Ocean.

1. What do you think the words on the medallion mean?

2. What other words or phrases could be used to get the medallion's message across?

3. Is the medallion effective in getting sympathy? Why or why not?

Name: _____

Unit 4 Lesson 6

Samuel Sewall
1652–1730

Samuel Sewall was born in England. He and his family settled Massachusetts, in 1661. Sewall was a successful merchant and was also a judge. Sewall wrote a pamphlet called *The Selling of Joseph*. Published in 1700, it was the first anti-slavery writing to be published in New England.

Below is an excerpt from what Sewall wrote. As you read, think about Sewall's arguments against slavery. What reasons does he give for opposing slavery?

"It is most certain that all men . . . have equal right unto liberty, and all other outward comforts of Life. It is . . . most lamentable [very sad] to think how, in taking Negroes out of Africa, and selling them here, that which God has joined together men boldly rent asunder [tear apart]; men from their country, husbands from their wives, parents from their children. How horrible is the uncleanness, mortality [death], if not murder, that the ships are guilty of that bring great crowds of these miserable men and women. Methinks when we are bemoaning [complaining about] the barbarous usage [terrible treatment] of our friends and kinfolk [white people] in Africa, [we should ask] whether we are not culpable [guilty] in forcing the Africans to become slaves among ourselves."

Name: _____

What was the role of slavery in colonial America?

1. 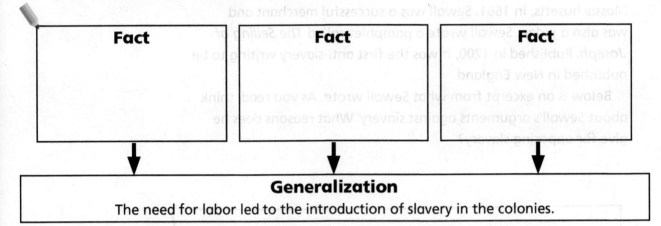 **Make Generalizations:** Fill in the chart below with facts that lead to the generalization about slavery in the colonies.

Fact	Fact	Fact

Generalization

The need for labor led to the introduction of slavery in the colonies.

2. *Understand* Describe the hardships that enslaved Africans faced on their journey from West Africa to the English colonies.

_____

_____

3. *Analyze* How were enslaved people treated differently from indentured servants?

_____

_____

4. *Evaluate* Why do you think some colonists were **proponents** of slavery? Why did others want enslaved people to **rebel**? Explain your answer.

_____

_____

5. **Write a Paragraph** Read the quotations from Olaudah Equiano's autobiography on page 92. Write a paragraph about what you think was the most interesting part of his writing and why.

Link to ••• **Math** Research the population total for enslaved people in the colonies from 1600–1850. Make a graph to show how the population of enslaved Africans grew during that time period.

Lesson 6 Assessment

Answers

1.

Fact	Fact	Fact
Plantations in the South grew.	Large plantations needed more workers.	Many Southerners favored and encouraged slavery.

↓ ↓ ↓

Generalization

The need for labor led to the introduction of slavery in the colonies.

2. They came on overcrowded ships, endured hunger, thirst, cruel treatment, and disease. Many died, and survivors lost all hope of returning home.

3. Enslaved people were considered property, bought and sold at auctions. They were punished by their owners if they disobeyed, and were not paid for their work. Indentured servants had to work for a set period of time in exchange for housing, food, and the cost of their voyage.

4. Possible answer: Many proponents were plantation owners who needed workers. Those who wanted the slaves to rebel had strong feelings about equal rights, freedom, and liberty.

5. Students' paragraphs should provide a quote from Equiano's diary and a concise explanation of why it is interesting. Use the following response to literature rubric to score students' paragraphs:

4	Student writes a paragraph that includes a quote and concise explanation. Spelling and grammar are correct.
3	Student writes a paragraph with a quote but explanation is incomplete. Spelling and grammar may have a few errors.
2	Student writes a paragraph without a quote and with an incomplete explanation. Spelling and grammar have some serious errors.
1	The sentences are not organized in a paragraph, there is no quote, and the explanation is incomplete. There are many serious errors.

Link to Math Students' graphs should reflect the growing population of enslaved people.

Intervention

Reading Skill Mini-Lesson　　ELA 5RC2.4

Reread the first paragraph on p. 91. Remind students that a generalization gives readers the "big picture." Ask students to look for facts that support the generalization: "The need for labor led to the introduction of slavery in the colonies."

Analysis Skill Mini-Lesson　　HI 2

Help students identify the human and physical characteristics of the South by helping them understand why there would be proponents of slavery and pointing out the need for labor on large plantations. Tell students that those who opposed slavery valued equal rights and thought it was wrong to own people as if they were property.

Writing Skill Mini-Lesson　　ELA 5WA2.2

Tell students that a good response to literature includes concise explanations that support one's position about the subject matter. Ask students to think about what it would have been like to be an enslaved person in colonial America. Brainstorm with the class reactions and feelings they might have had.

Math Support　　MNS1.1

Direct students to reference materials to find information on the slave population for this period.

What brought on democratic ideas in colonial America?

California Objective H-SS 5.4.7 Explain the early democratic ideas and practices that emerged during the colonial period, including the significance of representative assemblies and town meetings.

STANDARDS TRACE	
Introduce	Reinforce
pp. **93**T4, **93–96**	pp. **96**T1–T5, **141–144**

✓ **Core Instruction**	**Alternate Instruction**	
Content Paths		

Core Instruction

△ **Text Path,** p. **93**T4
Student Text, pp. **93–96**
Citizenship: Colonial and U.S. Governments

Alternate Instruction

📝 **Digital Path,** p. **96**T1
Video: *Colonial Democracies*

✋ **Active Path,** pp. **96**T2–T4
Colonial Williamsburg
Activity: Create a Colonial Government

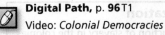

Big Ideas

Students Will Learn

Early colonial governments were set up to help solve problems and make rules.

Simple democractic governments were formed, inspired by England's House of Commons.

There were limits to colonial democracies.

Teacher Background

The Mayflower Compact of 1620 was created partly to discourage members of the group from leaving Plymouth to settle their own communities. The signers were bound to the colony so that a government could be formed, and it bound them to any laws that would be established later. When order could not be established in the early colonial days, martial law was used. The formation of governments helped to reduce the use of martial law, where the military enforces order without due process.

The House of Burgesses began as an agency of the Virginia Company in 1619. It soon grew to be the first elective body of self government in the colonies. By 1630 the House of Burgesses had led the decision of Virginia residents to grow and export tobacco without financial support from the Virginia Company or other English sources. Town meetings were established in the Massachusetts charter. In Boston a meeting room above Faneuil Hall Market was set up in 1742 to hold town meetings where citizens debated issues, elected town officials, voted on local taxes, and spent tax money. Today town meetings are still held in Faneuil Hall.

Common Misconception: Students may think that the United States "invented" representative government, and that it never existed before. England's House of Commons is one example, with limitations. American Indian groups were usually democracies where group decisions were made on many issues, notably on who would be the chief. In ancient Rome and Greece, certain people could elect senators or representatives.

Although colonists in North America did not have the right to vote for members of the British Parliament, Parliament still had the ability to pass laws for the colonists. The Magna Carta is a document that was written in 1215, which granted rights to English people. It later became the foundation for the constitutions of English-speaking countries. The document outlines issues such as limiting taxes and allowing all merchants arriving in England to be "free from all evil tolls . . ." Despite this promise, Britain taxed colonists heavily for trading activity.

Reading Transparency R20

🔄 **Make Generalizations** Use the transparency before teaching the lesson to generalize that *early settlers worked together to make fair laws for the colonies.*

Root Words Have students recall that root words are the main parts of words. Guide students to determine that *govern* is the root of *government.* Another word is *governor.*

Audio Student Text

[digital] ◀》 A digital audio version of the Student Text is available for students needing auditory support.

Introduce Lesson Vocabulary

For definitions, see p. 93. Read the words and definitions together. Ask students to take turns choosing a vocabulary card and recalling the definition aloud.

democracy	citizen
representative	assembly
town meeting	county seat

[digital] Lesson Pretest

• Ongoing Assessment pp. **93**T4, **96**T1, **96**T2

• Lesson Assessment p. **96**T6

[digital] Lesson Quiz

English Learners

Democracy Help students understand features of a *democracy.*

Beginning (Level 1): Have students choose an issue that is important to them. Then have them vote on the issue to model the choices common in a *democracy.*

Intermediate (Levels 2–3): Ask students if they think their class is a *democracy.* Help them determine that it is not because they do not get to choose what takes place.

Advanced (Levels 4–5): Have students discuss why they do or do not think *democracy* is the best form of government.

[digital] ◀》 Audio Student Text

Extra Support

Explain Have students write a brief paragraph explaining how the terms *democracy, citizen,* and *representation* relate to the concept of building a government that is run by the people.

Make Generalizations Have students make generalizations about how the governments of the American colonies carried out democracy.

[digital] ◀》 Audio Student Text

Inclusion/Special Needs

Build Background Discuss with students how democracy works today in the United States. Discuss how leaders are chosen and how different laws and decisions are made. Discuss how a democracy is different from a dictatorship or other forms of government which are not run by the citizens.

Model Concepts Conduct a mock town hall meeting with students. Decide on the issues that should be discussed and how the meeting will be conducted so that all voices are heard. Choose someone to be in charge of the meeting and discuss their role as the leader.

[digital] ◀》 Audio Student Text

Challenge

Compare and Contrast Lead a discussion with students about how the democracy of the American colonies was similar to and different from democracy in the United States today. Discuss how modern technology affects the opportunities for all citizens to be involved in the democratic process.

Analyze and Evaluate Review this statement from the lesson with students: "Colonial governments were not complete democracies." Discuss the meaning of this statement and then lead a debate about whether or not we have a complete democracy today or whether complete democracy can ever be achieved.

LESSON 7 What brought on democratic ideas in colonial America?

🐻 H-SS 5.4.7

Pacing	Materials	Assessment
35 MINUTES	· Student Text, pp. **93–96** · Student Text Transparencies, pp. **93–96** · *Find Out More* Handout, p. **96** T5	· `digital` Lesson Pretest · Lesson Assessment, p. **96** T6 · `digital` Lesson Quiz

1 Build Background

Activate Prior Knowledge Suggest a scenario in which the principal has made an unpopular decision, such as not allowing recess or banning classroom computers. Ask students how they feel about the principal making a decision that affects them without asking their opinions. Have the class vote whether to support the decision.

Preview the Lesson Read *Set the Scene* with the class. Have students study the picture, then describe the kind of people in the picture and what they are probably doing. Review

the classroom rules with students. Remind students that such rules help the classroom run efficiently. Tell students they will find out how the developing colonies established rules so they could function smoothly.

Introduce Vocabulary After students complete the vocabulary activity on p. 93, invite them to share what they think it means to live in a democracy and write some of their points on the board.

2 Teach

Read Together (pp. **94–95**) After each section, pause to discuss the lesson question "What brought on democratic ideas in colonial America?" and how the section helps answer that question.

Reading Informational Text As students read, point out the sequence of events. Point out that the House of Burgesses began meeting in Virginia (1619) before the Pilgrims arrived in Plymouth (1620).

`digital` 🔊 **Audio Student Text**

Summarize As students write their answers to the Lesson Summary on p. 95, remind them that a thorough summary should include different examples of democratic governments.

Find Out More (p. **96** T5) Have students read the page and then discuss why education is so important to a democratic form of government.

Citizenship: Colonial and U.S. Governments
`CST 3` (p. **96**) After completing the diagram, have students summarize the differences between colonial governments and our present-day U.S. government. Discuss why our present-day government is more democratic.

Ongoing *Assessment* ★

▶ **IF** students have trouble understanding how the colonies were not complete democracies (Question 4),

▶ **THEN** remind them that to be a complete democracy, all people who live in a community must have a say in how the community is governed. In colonial governments, only men who owned land could vote or become representatives. That meant that women and people who could not afford to own land had no say in creating the laws they had to obey.

3 Assess and Extend

Lesson Assessment (p. **96** T6)

Extend Reread the last paragraph on p. 95. Then have students predict what problems might arise because of British limitations on colonial democracy.

Name:

H-SS 5.4.7 Explain the early democratic ideas and practices that emerged during the colonial period, including the significance of representative assemblies and town meetings.

Lesson 7

What brought on democratic ideas in colonial America?

SET THE SCENE Have you and your friends ever taken a vote? Asking for everyone's opinion is one way to settle problems in a fair, organized way. When the colonists created governments, they wanted people to have a voice in making the laws. How did these ideas come about?

Preview the Lesson
Vocabulary

democracy *(n.)* a government that is run by the people

citizen *(n.)* a member of a country

representative *(n.)* a person who is chosen to act for others

assembly *(n.)* a gathering of elected representatives for a specific purpose

town meeting *(n.)* a gathering of people who live in a town to discuss issues

county seat *(n.)* a place where a county government is located

Vocabulary Activity Words we do not know often contain parts that we do know. Circle a familiar word with at least 8 letters in the vocabulary word *representative*. Write a definition for that word below.

to act for others

⊙ Reading: Make Generalizations

Generalizations are broad statements that are true for many people, places, or events. As you read the first section on page 94, underline a sentence that makes a generalization about the purposes of early colonial governments.

▷

93

LESSON 7 Overview

LESSON 7 Text Path

LESSON 7 Digital Path

LESSON 7 Active Path

LESSON 7 Assessment

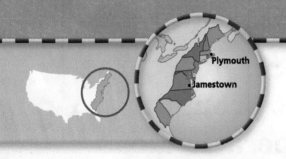

Early Colonial Government

Early American settlements needed governments to help solve problems and make rules. For example, in its first years, the Jamestown colony struggled for survival until governor Thomas Dale took charge and created strict new rules. Settlers were punished if they came late to work or broke tools. Before the Pilgrims landed in Plymouth, they drew up a document called the Mayflower Compact. In 1620 forty-one men signed the Compact, swearing to make "just and equal laws . . . for the general good of the Colony." This document became the basis of their government.

Government by the People

Many colonies formed governments based on the ideas of democracy. A **democracy** is a government that is run by the people. In a democracy, members of a country, called **citizens,** rule themselves. They can vote for and serve as representatives. **Representatives** are people who are chosen to act for others.

The idea of having representatives was similar to a part of government the colonists had known in England. The House of Commons was a group of elected representatives that passed laws and advised the king. Members of the House of Commons represented landholders and other property owners in England.

1. Make Generalizations **What generalization can you make about the Mayflower Compact?**

The purpose of the Mayflower Compact was to form the basis of the Pilgrims' government.

2. How were many colonial governments like the government the colonists had known in England? *Compare and Contrast*

The colonists wanted a government of representatives who would act for them, just as the House of Commons did in England.

Pilgrim men signed a document that set up a government for their colony while still at sea aboard their ship, the *Mayflower*.

94 • Life in the Colonies

Colonial Democracy

Throughout the colonies, people set up colonial governments in which they could have a voice in making the laws. Many colonies had an **assembly,** or a gathering of elected representatives for a specific purpose. At colonial assemblies, representatives made laws. The first colonial assembly, the House of Burgesses, met in Jamestown, Virginia, in 1619. Each settlement in Virginia sent two representatives to the assembly. There, "all matters [were] decided, determined and ordered by the greater part of the voices present."

Colonists also formed local governments. In New England, a gathering of people who lived in a town discussed issues at a **town meeting.** In the Southern Colonies, local representatives met at the **county seat,** the place where the county government was located.

The Limits of Colonial Democracies

Colonial governments were not complete democracies. There were limits on who could help run the government and what an assembly could do. Only white men who owned property could vote or be elected representatives. In addition, the British government could pass laws for the colonies without asking the opinions of the colonists. This last issue would cause serious problems in the years to come.

Summary Answer The colonies in Jamestown and Plymouth established governments to set rules and solve problems. Many of the colonists wanted a representative government similar to the one in England. Many colonies had assemblies where representatives met to make laws. Local governments held town meetings in New England or gathered at the county seat in the Southern Colonies.

3. Make Generalizations
Underline a generalization in the first paragraph about the kind of governments people set up in the colonies.

Twenty-two representatives from eleven settlements met in Virginia's first colonial assembly.

4. Underline ways that colonial governments were not complete democracies. *Main Idea and Details*

Summary

Early American colonies set up governments called democracies. How did democracies develop throughout the colonies?

LESSON 7 Overview
LESSON 7 Text Path
LESSON 7 Digital Path
LESSON 7 Active Path
LESSON 7 Assessment

Colonial and U.S. Governments

Learn More The system of government in the English colonies combined control by a king or queen with representative democracy. The king of England was the official ruler of the colonies. However, because he ruled from so far away, the king appointed governors to each colony to carry out his orders. Many colonial governments also had assemblies of elected representatives. These assemblies represented the interests of the colonists rather than those of the king.

Today, the United States is an independent country. Our system of government is a representative democracy that allows citizens to become more involved in their government. Unlike colonial government, our national government allows the people to help elect their President, who heads the country. The elected assemblies of the U.S. government, however, are similar to those in the colonies. Then and now, citizens elect representatives to serve their interests in governments.

The diagram below compares and contrasts colonial and U.S. governments. Complete the chart using these directions.

1. Complete the diagram by filling in the blanks. *Apply*

2. Circle the name of the government in which people could be more involved. *Analyze*

Colonial Government   **U.S. Government**

Both

- The ___king___ heads all of the colonies.
- Governors are ___appointed___ by the king.

- The people elect ___representatives___ to serve their interests in government.

- The ___President___ heads the country.
- State governors are elected by the citizens of that state.

Digital Path

LESSON 7 **What brought on democratic ideas in colonial America?**

H-SS 5.4.7

Path Prep	Pacing	Materials	Assessment
	50 MINUTES	· Video: *Colonial Democracies* · Interactive Practice: *Colonial Democracy Begins* · Print Partner: *Democracy Is Born* · **digital** ◀)) Audio Student Text	· **digital** Lesson Pretest · Lesson Assessment, p. **96** T6 · **digital** Lesson Quiz

1 Build Background

Activate Prior Knowledge Read aloud the dictionary definition of the word *democracy*. Have volunteers restate the definition in their own words. Explain that the United States government is run by its people through the leaders they elect by voting.

Introduce Vocabulary Introduce the lesson vocabulary words using the print or digital cards.

Lesson Introduction Launch the Lesson Introduction, which asks the question, "What brought on democratic ideas in colonial America?"

2 Teach

Video As students view *Colonial Democracies,* have them consider these questions:
• What is a democracy?
• What ideas or principles is it based on?
• What were the responsibilities of the different colonial governing bodies?

Interactive Practice Launch the activity, *Colonial Democracy Begins.* The activity will help students understand the foundations upon which colonial government was based.

Print Partner In this activity, students will complete a chart related to the birth of democracy in colonial America.

digital ◀)) **Audio Student Text**

Ongoing *Assessment* ★

▶ **IF** students are struggling to understand how a government is "run by the people,"

▶ **THEN** remind students that people run the government by voting in elections. Explain that through voting, people choose officials who will best represent their opinions and ideas; if a person wants changes in the government, he or she simply votes for the person who wants—and is willing to fight for— the same kinds of changes.

3 Assess and Extend

digital **Lesson Quiz** Have students check their lesson comprehension by completing the quiz. When students are finished, review the correct answers with the class.

Lesson Assessment Use the assessment on p. **96** T6 to evaluate students' progress.

Extend Organize the class into four groups. Explain that in the 1600s several plans of government were written for different colonies in America. Assign each group one of the following: Mayflower Compact, Fundamental Orders of Connecticut, Maryland Toleration Act, and Pennsylvania Frame of Government. Have students locate their government plan online and work together to translate it into "modern English." Invite the groups to read aloud their translations in class. After the readings, invite students to comment on how these plans of government may have helped to bring about democratic ideas in the colonies.

Active Path

Colonial Williamsburg

LESSON 7 What brought on democratic ideas in colonial America?

H-SS 5.4.7

Description: Students will create a colonial government to learn about the democratic ideas and practices of the colonial period.

Path Prep	Pacing	Materials	Assessment
	TWO 50-MINUTE SESSIONS	• 3 x 5 index cards • Writing paper • Handouts, pp. **96** T3–T4	• [digital] Lesson Pretest • Lesson Assessment, p. **96** T6 • [digital] Lesson Quiz

1 Build Background

Activate Prior Knowledge Make one card for each student. [Note: If there are thirty students in your class, write the words "enslaved person or indentured servant" on fifteen cards, "woman" on eight cards, "worker" on three cards, and "landowner" on four cards.] Shuffle the cards and give one to each student. Have students stand. Tell everyone with "enslaved person or indentured servant" cards to sit. Tell everyone with

"woman" cards to sit. Finally tell everyone with "worker" cards to sit. Only students with "landowner" cards remain standing. Explain that during the colonial period only white men who owned property were allowed to vote and participate in government.

Introduce Vocabulary Preview the vocabulary on p. 93.

2 Teach

Introduce Activity Explain to students that they will create a colonial government and that, for the purposes of this activity, everyone will be a "landowner." In colonial America, town meetings and legislative assemblies helped colonial Americans shape ideas about how government should work.

Activity Steps

1. Explain that the classroom is now an English colony and you, the teacher, are the king. Use the *Colonial Government Situation Cards* handout and the *Colonial Government Teacher Instructions* handout, to guide the activity.

2. On a piece of paper, have students write down three things that Americans learned about government during the colonial period. *(How to hold elections, run a legislature, that the king or executive should not have unlimited power, etc.)*

Ongoing *Assessment* ★

▶ **IF** students have problems understanding the role of the king,

▶ **THEN** explain that the king was the unelected head of the English government, including all the colonial governments.

3 Assess and Extend

Assess Assessment is based on student participation in the activity and the quality of their written assignment. Writing should clearly demonstrate an understanding of colonial government.

Lesson Assessment (p. **96** T6)

Extend Have students come up with a list of things they think Americans did not learn well enough during the colonial period about how a government should be run. Have them explain why they made their selections.

 *Colonial Williamsburg*

Colonial Government Situation Cards

Instructions for the Sheriff

You are the county sheriff. It is your responsibility to hold the election for representatives to the colonial assembly. This is not a secret ballot. Every student must stand up and declare the name of the person for whom he or she is voting.

1. Stand in the front of the room and write the names of the candidates on the board.

2. Call out the name of each student one at a time. Ask students to stand and say out loud the name of the person for whom they are voting.

3. Count the number of votes that each candidate receives. The five candidates with the most votes are the winners of the election.

4. Announce the winners of the election to the class.

Instructions for the Assembly Card 1

If the king tries to tax you, write a protest (called a "petition") to the king. The protest should say why you think the tax is unfair. Try to get the assembly to approve the protest. Send the protest to the governor and ask the governor to send it to the king.

Instruction for the Assembly Card 2

Pass a law that says the class should have one hour for lunch. Give the bill to the governor and ask him and the council to approve it. Remember that you can pass bills and make decisions, but they are not official unless the governor, council, and king approve them.

Instruction for the Governor and Council Card 1

You have decided that the assembly needs to meet and determine how long students should have for lunch. Write out a proclamation that says, "I have decided that it is time for the assembly to meet. The sheriff should hold an election. After the election Representatives should meet to consider how long students should have for lunch. I give this order in the name of the king, [sign your name]."

Instruction for the Governor and Council Card 2

If the assembly gives you a protest (called a "petition") to the king, or a law, you must decide if it is fair and wise. If you think the protest or bill is fair, then send it to the king. If you disagree with the protest or bill, send it back to the assembly and tell them you do not approve and will not send it to the king. Remember that the king must approve every law passed by the assembly.

 *Colonial Williamsburg*

Colonial Government Teacher Instructions

1. Appoint one student as governor. Select three students to be the governor's advisors and one student to be the county sheriff. Make sure students understand that it is the king's right to appoint certain government officials. Give the governor and council the "Instructions for the Governor and Council" card 1.

2. Give the sheriff the "Instructions for the Sheriff" card. Help the class nominate a slate of candidates. Allow the sheriff to conduct the election according to the instruction sheet and select, by vote, five students for the assembly.

3. Inform students that you are the king and that you have worked very hard to make sure that your classroom is a safe and educational place for all of them. That work has been expensive and so you have decided to tax them. You expect each student to give you one piece of paper. Walk around the room and collect one piece of paper from every student.

4. Give the members of the assembly "Instructions for the Assembly" card 1. Give them time to protest the tax and give the protest to the governor. Have the governor and council discuss the protest and decide if it should be given to the king. If they give it to you, simply reply that you are the king and can do whatever you want.

5. Give the members of the assembly "Instructions for the Assembly" card 2. Give them time to develop their law and send it to the governor and council for their approval. Once the governor and council approve it, have them send it to you. Inform the governor that it does not matter what the assembly has decided because you do not like this bill and will not allow it to become law.

6. Use this activity to start a class discussion. Ask students: *What kinds of things do you think colonial Americans learned about governing themselves?* Guide the conversation to include items such as: hold elections, run a legislature, that the king (or executive) should not have unlimited power, that voting should be available for more people, that government officials should be elected and not appointed, etc.

Unit 4 Lesson 7

Education in a Democratic Society

You have read about how important self-government and democratic ideas were to the colonists. Many colonial leaders believed that if self-government and democratic ideas were going to work in the colonies, people needed to be educated and able to read and write.

In 1636 the Massachusetts Bay Colony, under the leadership of its governor John Winthrop, founded Harvard College. In 1642 the colony passed a law stating that everyone must be able to read. Five years later, it set up its first public schools. Between 1650 and 1776, the literacy rate in New England grew from about fifty percent to about ninety percent. Today Harvard is the oldest university in the country.

In 1731 Benjamin Franklin started the first public lending library in the colonies. Many years later, another leader in American education, Horace Mann, would say, "If we do not prepare children to become good citizens, if we do not develop their capacities [abilities], if we do not enrich their minds with knowledge then our republic must go down to destruction . . . "

With a partner discuss why you think education is important in a democratic society. If people are not educated, how might a democratic society "go down to destruction"?

In 1791 the library that Franklin started moved into this building in Philadelphia.

What brought on democratic ideas in colonial America?

1. ⊙ **Make Generalizations:** Read the facts below. Then make a generalization based on those facts to complete the chart.

Fact	**Fact**	**Fact**
Virginia representatives met at the House of Burgesses.	New England colonists held town meetings.	Local representatives in Southern Colonies met at the county seat.

↓ ↓ ↓

Generalization

2. *Understand* In the earliest English settlements, how did the need for survival lead to setting up governments?

_____

_____

3. *Analyze* In what ways did the colonies have representative governments? In what ways were the governments not representative?

_____

_____

4. *Evaluate* In what ways was a **democracy** better than the government run by a king and queen?

_____

_____

5. **Write a Letter** You are a colonist who does not own any land. Write a persuasive letter to the local newspaper about why **citizens** who do not own land should be allowed to vote.

Link to ∽∞∽ Math Working with a partner, determine an issue on which to conduct a survey of your class. Tally the results of your survey and determine the percentage of students who would vote for each side of the issue.

Lesson 7 Assessment

Answers

1.

Fact	Fact	Fact
Virginia representatives met at the House of Burgesses.	New England colonists held town meetings.	Local representatives in Southern Colonies met at the county seat.

↓ ↓ ↓

Generalization

Throughout the colonies, people wanted governments in which they could make their own laws.

2. Settlers needed governments to help solve problems and make rules.

3. Representative: Some colonies had assemblies and others had local governments. Not representative: Only white men who owned property could vote, and the British could pass laws on the colonies.

4. A democracy allows adult citizens to take part in government by voting for officials, while the English government was ruled by a monarch and the members of the House of Commons only represented landowners.

5. Letters should be persuasive and contain logical reasons for allowing non-property owners the right to vote. Use the following persuasive writing rubric to score students' letters:

4	Student writes a multiple-paragraph letter that contains logical and persuasive reasons. Spelling and grammar are correct.
3	Student writes one or two paragraphs that include some logical and persuasive reasons. Spelling and grammar may have a few errors.
2	Student writes a one-paragraph letter that includes some logical reasons but lacks persuasiveness. Spelling and grammar have some serious errors.
1	Letter is not organized as a paragraph. It has no logical reasons and is not persuasive. There are many serious errors.

Link to Math Students' percentages should accurately reflect the results of their tallies.

Intervention

Reading Skill Mini-Lesson ELA 5RC2.4

Review with students that a generalization is a statement that is true for most people. Go back into the text and reread "Colonial Democracy." Have students find the facts listed in the chart. Then have them form a statement that is true for all the colonies.

Analysis Skill Mini-Lesson CST 3

Point out that although we enjoy a democracy now, the early colonies were still very much under the rule of England. Only landowners could vote, and England often imposed laws on the colonists without their consent.

Writing Skill Mini-Lesson ELA 5WA2.4

Tell students that a good persuasive letter includes logical justifications so readers will react favorably. Ask students to think about what position they will take, and what details they will use to support their position. Remind them that a persuasive letter is well organized.

Math Support MNS1.2

Help students choose an appropriate issue and allow pairs of students to interview their classmates or submit a written opinion poll to them.

Unit 4 Notes for Next Year

FIELD TRIP IDEAS

Location: _____

_____

Contact: _____

_____

Phone: _____

Location: _____

_____

Contact: _____

_____

Phone: _____

FIELD TRIP IDEAS

Additional Thoughts

BOOKS, VIDEOS, SOFTWARE

www. _____

www. _____

www. _____

www. _____

www. _____

www. _____

www. _____

Favorite Web Sites

Grade 5

Unit 4

Life in the Colonies
Resources

Reading Support

Content Readers	**96**T10
Read-Aloud Literature	**96**T11
Bibliography	**96**T12

Content Support

School-to-Home Newsletters (English and Spanish)	**96**T13
Time Line Card Masters	**96**T15
Vocabulary Card Masters	**96**T17
Biography Card Masters	**96**T23

Assessment

Culminating Writing	**96**T27
Multiple-Choice	**96**T31
Short-Answer	**96**T34
Answer Key	**96**T37

The Jamestown Colony

Each of these books focuses on the first permanent English settlement in North America—Jamestown. The unit's target reading skill, *Make Generalizations,* is addressed as readers use the text and prior knowledge to discover commonalities among people, places, or events. The vocabulary words listed in each book assist in students' comprehension of the material. Leveled activities for each of the three books are listed below. Most of these activities correspond to the reading skill in the Student Text.

Below Level

Jamestown

Before Reading Give students a chance to preview the book. Ask the following questions: *What do you know about the settlement of Jamestown? What do you know about John Smith and Pocahontas?* Allow time for discussion.

During Reading Remind students to look for clue words such as *many, most,* and *sometimes* to signal generalizations. On p. 8, have students identify the clue words and the generalizations that are made.

After Reading Encourage students to compare the generalizations they identified with facts from the text. Then have students determine the difference between a generalization and a fact.

On Level

The Jamestown Colony

Before Reading Give students a chance to preview the book. Ask them if they can make any generalizations just by looking at the images.

During Reading In the text box on p. 14, have students determine the generalization that is being made. Have them identify the clue word that helped determine the generalization.

After Reading Discuss with students the problems faced by the Jamestown settlers and how they solved them. Encourage students to evaluate the solutions.

Above Level

John Smith and the Survival of Jamestown

Before Reading As students preview the book, have them make generalizations about life in the early colonies. Encourage them to discuss what they already know about the Jamestown settlement and what they hope to find out by reading the book.

During Reading On p. 5, have students identify the clue word that signals the generalization about Algonquian words. Then have them discuss why colonists used so many Algonquian words.

After Reading Ask students to discuss the historical figures associated with Jamestown and to evaluate the importance of the settlement. Why was the establishment of this colony important? What conclusions can they draw about John Smith's character?

Read-Aloud Literature

The Pilgrims of Plimoth

by Marcia Sewall

(New York: Simon & Schuster,
ISBN 0-689-80861-5, 1986)
Nonfiction

In 1620 a group of Separatists sailed from Plymouth, England, on the *Mayflower*. Most were Pilgrims seeking religious freedom; some sought wealth instead. After about two months at sea, they landed at present-day Cape Cod and elected their first governor, thereby officially beginning a new life in America. *The Pilgrims of Plimoth* chronicles the hardships, successes, and daily life of the Pilgrims during their first year at Plymouth, with sections devoted to the responsibilities of

"menfolk," "womenfolk," and "children and youngfolk." The events covered include the establishment of a colony at Plimoth (Plymouth), the Pilgrims' relations with American Indians, the development of their agricultural skills, and their efforts to maintain their religious traditions in this new land. The Pilgrims' story is told from the first-person perspective of an unnamed member of the colony, with diction and syntax resembling that of seventeenth-century language. Also included is a glossary defining some of the more vernacular terms used by Pilgrims during this era. Overall, Marcia Sewall's text and illustrations provide an intimate look into the life of these early colonists.

Related Titles

Jamestown, by James E. Knight. (Scholastic, ISBN 0-439-63587-X, 2004) Fiction
A grandfather tells his grandchildren about being one of the original Jamestown colonists.
Below Grade Level

William Penn: Founder of the Pennsylvania Colony, by Bernadette L. Baczynski. (Capstone Press, ISBN 0-736-82459-6, 2004) Biography
The Quaker William Penn made peace with American Indians and provided religious freedom within the Pennsylvania colony.
Below Grade Level

Roanoke: The Lost Colony: An Unsolved Mystery from History, by Jane Yolen and Heidi Elisabet Yolen Stemple. (Simon & Schuster Books for Young Readers, ISBN 0-689-82321-5, 2003) Fiction
Readers can study clues and theories about the mysterious disappearance of the Roanoke colonists and form their own conclusions about what might have happened.
On Grade Level

Williamsburg, by Judy Alter. (Compass Point Books, ISBN 0-756-50300-0, 2002) Nonfiction
Williamsburg's history is covered in this book, from its founding and establishment as Virginia's capital to its restoration as a living museum.
On Grade Level

James Towne: Struggle for Survival, by Marcia Sewall. (Simon & Schuster Children's Publishing, ISBN 0-689-81814-9, 2001) Nonfiction
From the viewpoint of one of its settlers, Jamestown's early days are recounted in this book.
Above Grade Level

Stranded at Plimouth Plantation 1626, by Gary Bowen. (HarperCollins Publishers, ISBN 0-064-40719-5, 1998) Fiction
This fictional diary of a thirteen-year-old boy details life in a Pilgrim colony.
Above Grade Level

Bibliography

Student Resources

These titles will assist fifth grade students in learning about life during the colonial era. These titles may be available at your local library media center.

If You Lived in Williamsburg in Colonial Days, by Barbara Brenner. (Scholastic, ISBN 0-590-92922-4, 2000) Nonfiction
This book describes life in Williamsburg, Virginia, over 200 years ago.
Below Grade Level

Who Owns the Sun? by Stacy Chbosky. (Landmark Editions, ISBN 0-933-84914-1, 1998) Fiction
This story, written by a fourteen-year-old, tells of a boy who learns that much of the world cannot be owned by anyone, yet he and his father are enslaved.
Below Grade Level

Ben Franklin of Old Philadelphia, by Margaret Cousins. (Random House Children's Books, ISBN 0-394-84928-0, 2004) Biography
This biography tells of Franklin's work as a printer, editor, inventor, statesman, and ambassador.
On Grade Level

Tituba of Salem Village, by Ann Petry. (HarperCollins Children's Book Group, ISBN 0-064-40403-X, 1991) Fiction
In 1692 an enslaved person from Barbados is suspected of being a witch in Salem, Massachusetts.
On Grade Level

Lord Baltimore: English Politician and Colonist, by Loree Lough. (Chelsea House Publishers, ISBN 0-791-05692-9, 1999) Biography
This book focuses on the Catholic baron who founded the Maryland colony.
Above Grade Level

To Be a Slave, by Julius Lester. (Penguin Group, ISBN 0-141-31001-4, 2000) Nonfiction
Coupling the words of enslaved people with Lester's commentary, this book provides a chronological compilation of the history of enslavement from leaving Africa through the early twentieth century.
Above Grade Level

Teacher Resources

Primary Sources Teaching Kit: Colonial America, by Karen Baicker. (Scholastic, ISBN 0-590-37847-3, 2002)
Primary sources on such topics as religion, daily life, government, and slavery in colonial America are included along with background information and teaching ideas.

Rules of Civility: The 110 Precepts That Guided Our First President in War and Peace, by George Washington. (University Press of Virginia, ISBN 0-813-92218-6, 2003)
Washington's rules of civility, which he copied into a notebook as a student, offer insight into the etiquette and society of the 1700s.

Writings: Poor Richard's Almanack; The Autobiography; Bagatelles, Pamphlets, Essays and Letters, by Benjamin Franklin. (The Library of America, ISBN 0-940-45029-1, 1987)
In addition to those writings mentioned in the title, this collection also includes Franklin's scientific papers and "The Whistle."

Internet Resources

 Web sites are subject to change. Make certain to review these Web sites before suggesting them to students.

http://library.thinkquest.org
Search for "Colonial Kids: A Celebration of Life in Southeastern Pennsylvania in the 1700s" to learn about colonial life and times from a kid's point of view.

http://www.history.org
This Web site of the Colonial Williamsburg Foundation includes articles, audio clips, teaching resources, electronic field trips, and more.

http://noahwebsterhouse.org
The Web site of the Noah Webster House Museum has information about Colonial amusements, including games, toys, tongue twisters, and riddles.

Visit the Scott Foresman Web site for online resources. Go to **cahistorysocialscience.com** where you will find biographies, U.S. and world maps, current news reports, an online dictionary and encyclopedia, and much more!

School-to-Home Newsletter

Scott Foresman History-Social Science for California

Unit 4: Life in the Colonies

History-Social Science 5.4 Students understand the political, religious, social, and economic institutions that evolved in the colonial era.

Here are the main ideas we are learning:

- Resources drew many English settlers to North America in the 1600s.

- Many Southern Colonies were founded as corporate and proprietary colonies.

- Many of the founders of New England Colonies had religious motives.

- The Middle Colonies were founded by Dutch, Swedish, and English settlers.

- The First Great Awakening in the 1700s, when some began to practice religion in new ways, was met with favor by some people and resistance by others.

- In the 1500s and 1600s, French colonists were fur traders and Spanish colonists had farms or ranches.

- English colonists were farmers or townspeople with jobs.

- Economic and government systems developed in different regions.

- First American Indians, then Africans, began to be enslaved to work in the Americas in the 1500s. Many people resisted slavery.

Family Activities

Talk Together

Discuss the difficulties colonists may have had as they established themselves in America. You might discuss the different languages, religions, kinds of educations, and desires that colonists had.

Learn Together

Help your child learn about the colonies.

- Read about one or more people who resisted slavery in the 1700s. What did they say or do to express their opposition?

- If possible, attend a reenactment of life during colonial times (or watch a movie that takes place in 18th-century America). Note the manners, dress, and speech of the characters.

- Compare the agricultural industries of the Southern Colonies with those that exist in those states today. Discuss why you think they are similar or different.

Read Together

If You Lived in Williamsburg in Colonial Days, by Barbara Brenner. (Scholastic, ISBN 0-590-92922-4, 2000) Nonfiction

Ben Franklin of Old Philadelphia, by Margaret Cousins. (Random House Children's Books, ISBN 0-394-84928-0, 2004) Biography

To Be a Slave, by Julius Lester. (Penguin Group, ISBN 0-141-31001-4, 2000, 2000) Nonfiction

Unit Reading Skill

Students are learning to Make Generalizations, or statements that are true for many people, places, or events. Generalizations are helpful because they explain the big picture.

THANK YOU for supporting your child's education!

Boletín **De la escuela al hogar**

Unidad 4: La vida en las colonias

Historia-Ciencias Sociales 5.4 Los estudiantes entienden las instituciones políticas, religiosas, sociales y económicas que se desarrollaron en la época colonial.

Éstas son las ideas principales que estamos estudiando:

- Los recursos naturales atrajeron a muchos colonos ingleses a América del Norte en el siglo XVII.

- Muchas de las Colonias del Sur fueron fundadas como colonias empresariales y de un solo propietario.

- Muchas de las colonias de Nueva Inglaterra fueron fundadas por motivos religiosos.

- Las Colonias Centrales fueron fundadas por colonos holandeses, suecos, e ingleses.

- El Primer Gran Despertar en el siglo XVIII, a partir del cual algunos comenzaron a practicar su religión de manera diferente, fue recibido con aprobación por unos y con resistencia por otros.

- En los siglos XVI y XVII, los colonos franceses eran comerciantes de pieles y los españoles tenían granjas y ranchos.

- Los colonos ingleses eran pequeños granjeros o trabajaban en empleos en las ciudades.

- Se desarrollaron sistemas económicos y gubernamentales en diferentes regiones.

- Primeramente los indígenas americanos, y más tarde los africanos, comenzaron a ser esclavizados para trabajar en las Américas en el siglo XVI. Mucha gente se resistió a la esclavitud.

Actividades en familia

Conversen juntos

Hablen de las dificultades que pueden haber confrontado los colonos cuando se establecieron en América. Pueden hablar de los distintos idiomas religiones, educaciones educativos y deseos que tenían los colonos.

Aprendan juntos

Ayude a su niño o su niña a aprender acerca de las colonias.

- Lean acerca de una o más personas que se resistieron a la esclavitud en el siglo XVIII. ¿Qué dijeron o hicieron para expresar su oposición?

- Si les es posible, visiten un museo viviente o representación teatral de la época colonial (o vean una película que tenga lugar en América del Norte en el siglo XIX). Observen los modales, vestimenta y forma de hablar de los actores. ¿En qué se diferencian de la apariencia y forma de actuar de los estadounidenses de hoy en día?

- Comparen las industrias agrícolas de las Colonias del Sur con las que existen en estos estados hoy en día. Comenten en qué se parecen o se diferencien.

Lean juntos

Benjamin Franklin: político e inventor estadounidense, por Maya Glasss. (Rosen Publishing, ISBN 0-823-94221X, 2004) No ficción

Sojourner Truth: defensora de los derechos civiles, por Kathleen Collins. (Rosen Publishing, ISBN 0-823-942392, 2004) No ficción

Betsy Ross: creadora de la bandera estadounidense, por Tracie Egan. (Rosen Publishing, ISBN 0-823-941523, 2003) No ficción

Destreza de lectura de la unidad

Los estudiantes están aprendiendo a hacer generalizaciones, o sea, afirmaciones que se pueden aplicar a mucha gente, muchos lugares o muchos acontecimientos. Las generalizaciones sirven para explicar la idea general.

Gracias por apoyar la educación de su niño o niña.

Time Line Cards

1607

Jamestown is founded in Virginia.

© Pearson Scott Foresman
Jamestown National Historic Park/National Park Service

1620

The Pilgrims found Plymouth Colony.

© Pearson Scott Foresman
SuperStock

1664

© Pearson Scott Foresman
The Granger Collection, NY

England captures New Netherlands and renames it New York.

1733

James Oglethorpe founds Georgia colony.

© Pearson Scott Foresman
Stock Montage Inc.

Vocabulary Cards

Unit 4, Lesson 1

plantation

Unit 4, Lesson 1

cash crop

Unit 4, Lesson 1

proprietor

Unit 4, Lesson 1

indentured servant

Unit 4, Lesson 1

self-sufficient

Unit 4, Lesson 1

grant

Unit 4, Lesson 2

persecution

Unit 4, Lesson 2

Separatists

Unit 4, Lesson 2

pilgrim

Unit 4, Lesson 2

Puritan

Vocabulary Cards

Unit 4, Lesson 1

(n.) a crop that is grown to be sold for profit

Unit 4, Lesson 1

(n.) a large farm with many workers who lived on the land they worked

Unit 4, Lesson 1

(n.) a person who agreed to work for an amount of time in exchange for the cost of housing, food, and the voyage to North America

Unit 4, Lesson 1

(n.) an owner

Unit 4, Lesson 1

(v.) to give something formally to someone

Unit 4, Lesson 1

(adj.) having the ability to produce most everything that one needs

Unit 4, Lesson 2

(n.) a group of people from England who wanted to separate themselves from the Church of England

Unit 4, Lesson 2

(n.) unjust treatment

Unit 4, Lesson 2

(n.) a person from England who wanted to improve the Church of England

Unit 4, Lesson 2

(n.) a person who travels to a place for religious reasons

Vocabulary Cards

Unit 4, Lesson 2

dissenter

Unit 4, Lesson 3

intolerant

Unit 4, Lesson 4

preacher

Unit 4, Lesson 5

artisan

Unit 4, Lesson 5

apprentice

Unit 4, Lesson 5

town common

Unit 4, Lesson 5

free-market economy

Unit 4, Lesson 6

auction

Unit 4, Lesson 6

proponent

Unit 4, Lesson 6

rebel

Vocabulary Cards

(adj.) to be not accepting of ideas or behaviors different from one's own	*(n.)* a person whose views are different from those of his or her leaders
(n.) a skilled worker who makes things by hand	*(n.)* a person who gives speeches about religious subjects
(n.) an open space in the center of a town where cattle and sheep could graze	*(n.)* a person who learns a skill or trade from an experienced worker
(n.) a public sale in which something is sold to the person who offers the most money	*(n.)* a system in which prices are not controlled by the government
(v.) to resist or fight against authority	*(n.)* a person who supports something

Vocabulary Cards

Unit 4, Lesson 7

democracy

Unit 4, Lesson 7

citizen

Unit 4, Lesson 7

representative

Unit 4, Lesson 7

assembly

Unit 4, Lesson 7

town meeting

Unit 4, Lesson 7

county seat

Vocabulary Cards

Unit 4, Lesson 7

(n.) a member of a country

Unit 4, Lesson 7

(n.) a government that is run by the people

Unit 4, Lesson 7

(n.) a gathering of elected representatives for a specific purpose

Unit 4, Lesson 7

(n.) a person who is chosen to act for others

Unit 4, Lesson 7

(n.) a place where a county government is located

Unit 4, Lesson 7

(n.) a gathering of people who live in a town to discuss issues

Biography Cards

Eliza Lucas Pinckney
1722–1793

John Smith
1579?–1631

Lord Baltimore
1605?–1675

James Oglethorpe
1696-1785

William Bradford
1590-1657

John Winthrop
1588-1649

Thomas Hooker
1586?-1647

Roger Williams
1603?-1683

Duke of York
1633-1701

Biography Cards

Founder of the colony of Maryland

- Founded the colony of Maryland in 1634 as a place for Catholics who were persecuted in England
- Sent his brother, Lenard Calvert, to govern the colony of Maryland

Lord Baltimore
1605?–1675

Helped establish the English colony of Jamestown

- Joined the expedition that founded Jamestown in 1607 and became the colony's leader
- Helped establish trade with the American Indians and claimed to have been rescued by Pocahontas

John Smith
1579?–1631

Colonist who managed the plantation that was the first to successfully grow indigo

- Raised the colonies' first successful crop of indigo, a plant used to make blue dye
- Managed three plantations in South Carolina

Eliza Lucas Pinckney
1722–1793

First governor of the Massachusetts Bay Colony

- Led a group of Puritans to Massachusetts so they could worship freely
- Helped found the Massachusetts Bay Colony and its main settlement, the city of Boston

John Winthrop
1588–1649

Governor of Plymouth Colony, the first permanent colony in New England

- Elected governor of Plymouth Colony in 1621 and helped write the Mayflower Compact
- Helped establish democratic practices such as voting and town meetings

William Bradford
1590–1657

Helped found Georgia, the last of the thirteen English colonies in North America

- Founded Georgia to give English debtors, or people who owed money, a new start as farmers
- Established peaceful relations with the American Indians

James Oglethorpe
1696–1785

King of England and for whom New York is named

- Sent the fleet that captured New Amsterdam from the Dutch in 1664 and renamed the colony New York
- Became King James II of England in 1685

Duke of York
1633–1701

Founder of the colony of Rhode Island

- Banned from Massachusetts Bay Colony because of his belief that government should not interfere in religious matters
- Founded the city of Providence in 1636 on land that he purchased from the Narragansett

Roger Williams
1603?–1683

Puritan clergyman who founded Hartford, Connecticut

- Founded Hartford in 1636 to escape the strict religious control of the Puritans
- Helped create the Fundamental Orders of Connecticut, which is considered to be the first written constitution

Thomas Hooker
1586?–1647

Biography Cards

William Penn
1644–1718

Anne Hutchinson
1591–1643

Jonathan Edwards
1703–1758

George Whitefield
1714–1770

Olaudah Equiano
1745–1797

Biography Cards

Puritan minister who helped bring about the First Great Awakening

- Wrote and gave sermons during the First Great Awakening about the dangers of people not having a strong faith

- Believed that people are free to do as they please but are responsible for their actions

Colonist who contributed to the idea of freedom of religion in Colonial America

- Sent away from Massachusetts Bay Colony by Puritan leaders for refusing to change her religious beliefs

- Co-founded Portsmouth, Rhode Island, in 1638

Founder of the colony of Pennsylvania

- Founded Pennsylvania in 1681 as a place where people of all religions and backgrounds could live together

- Established a democratic government and the first constitution that allowed for changes, or amendments

Free African American who wrote a book about his experiences as an enslaved person

- Published his autobiography in 1789, which showed the hardships of enslaved Africans

- Traveled to England where he became an abolitionist, working to end slavery

English preacher who traveled throughout the colonies during the First Great Awakening

- Began preaching tours in the colonies in 1739, and his dramatic sermons inspired new religious faith

- Preached in open fields to large crowds of both men and women

Write a Colonial Narrative

Description: Students will write a narrative letter from a young colonist to a friend or relative back in England.

Pacing	Materials	Assessment
⏱ 50 MINUTES	· Writing Tools, pp. **96**T29–T30 · Writing Transparencies, **W**7, **W**8	· Narrative Writing Rubric, pp. **96**T28

1 Build Background

Encourage students to discuss the things they might write about in a letter to a pen pal who lives in another country. What events in their lives would they want a pen pal to know about? What information about the student's life would a pen pal need in order to understand the importance of these events? Tell students that they will use their knowledge of the English colonial regions to write a narrative in the form of a letter from a young colonist who has recently arrived in North America to a relative or friend back in England.

2 Teach

Activity Steps

1. Use Writing Transparency **W**7 to review with students the skill of narrative writing.

2. Help students choose a colonial region to serve as the setting for their story. Tell them that the region they choose will provide details for their story's setting, characters, and plot.

3. Share the Story Map Writing Tool to help students brainstorm the elements of their story. Tell them to begin by completing the Where, Who, and When box. The Who should be a young person of about the students' age who has only recently arrived in the colonies from England. Students should also create another character who still lives back in England and who will receive a letter from the main character about an important event. Encourage students to think of details that will help guide the action and bring the story alive for readers. For example, a story set in New England may be very different if it is set in winter rather than in summer. You may want to direct students who set their stories in the Southern Colonies to place the action on a small farm rather than on a plantation holding enslaved people.

4. Help students complete the Story Map's Problem box. Tell students to think about an object or privilege they might want if they lived in this region during colonial times. Then have them think of a chore or other task that someone their age might perform in order to gain this object or privilege.

5. Direct students to complete the Story Map's Resolution box. Remind them that life in the colonies could be harsh and that their main character does not have to achieve what he or she hopes. Instead, the story could resolve with the character having a better understanding of his or her new home and what it will take to succeed next time.

6. Next, help students organize a beginning, middle, and end to their story in the Story Map's Main Events box. Ask: *What action shows the character forming a goal? What actions show the main character trying to reach their goal? What action will show the goal being met or missed?*

7. Finally, have students write a title for their story. Tell students that a good story title should include a specific detail to tell their readers where the story is set and what will happen, in a general way. For example, "Hard Times in New England" or "Philadelphia's Newest Apprentice."

8. Have students use the scaffolded My Colonial Story Model Writing Tool to write a first draft of their stories. Note that the story is written in the form of a letter. Point out that this model only asks them to develop part of their stories. Remind students that they will also write a full draft, in which they will add more details and events.

9. After students have written a full draft, have them exchange their work with a partner who has set his or her story in a different region. Tell students to use the Revise It! section on Writing Transparency **W**8 to review each other's work. Give students time to revise their work based on the feedback and to make a final copy of their story.

③ Assess and Extend

Assess Use the narrative writing rubric below to score student writing.

4	Student's story includes all narrative elements. The story has a clear sense of setting and character. The plot is built around a conflict that is developed in a clear beginning, middle, and end. The story includes many details that are appropriate to the chosen colonial region. Spelling and grammar are correct.
3	Student's story includes all narrative elements but does not have a clearly focused sense of setting or character. The story has inaccurate as well as accurate narrative details. Spelling and grammar may have a few errors.
2	The story's narrative elements occur in a poorly organized, unfocused way. There are some accurate details but key narrative information has been left out. Spelling and grammar have some serious errors.
1	Student's story leaves out most narrative elements. It has few or no narrative details. There are many serious spelling and grammar errors.

Extend Have students go to your library or media center to find out more about the lives of young people in their chosen colonial region. Have students research the clothes young people wore, their games and toys, and how they celebrated holidays and birthdays.

Name: _____

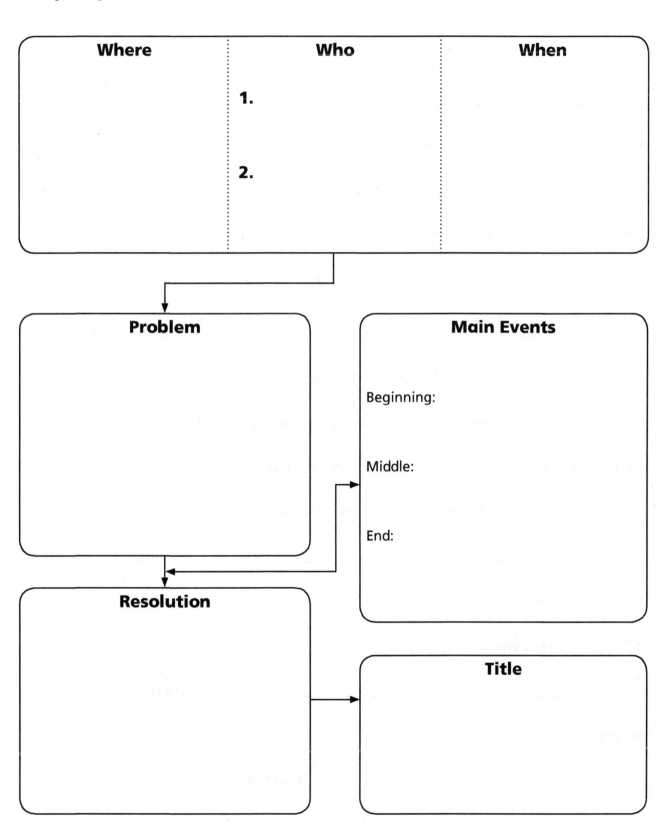

Where	Who	When
	1.	
	2.	

Problem

Main Events

Beginning:

Middle:

End:

Resolution

Title

Dear _____ :

How long has it been since I saw you last? I arrived in _____ only a few

months ago, and yet so much has happened in such a short time that it often feels like I have

been here for years! When we left _____ because _____

_____, who could have known that so much would change?

When we arrived in _____, Mother and Father and I moved into

a _____. Father quickly began working as a _____

_____ , while Mother had her hands full trying to set up a new house in a new world. She

also had her hands full taking care of me. I'm growing older and stronger every day, though, so

I thought that I too should start a new life here. I decided that I wanted to _____

_____. As you may have guessed, it

was easier to want to _____ than to actually accomplish it.

Still, I had a plan. I would _____

____ _____ until I achieved

my goal. . . .

Yours truly,

_____

Name: _____

Life in the Colonies

Directions: Fill in the circle next to the correct answer. Read the following paragraph to answer the first two questions.

(1) People came to North America for many reasons. (2) Many wanted an opportunity to start a new life and buy some land. (3) Others saw a chance to make money by finding gold or trading furs. (4) Some wanted to escape religious <u>persecution.</u> (5) They saw America as a place of tolerance and freedom.

1 Which of the following was *not* a reason to come to the colonies?

(A) to escape tolerance

(B) to own their own land

(C) to find religious freedom

(D) to work in the fur trade

2 What is the meaning of <u>persecution</u> in sentence 4?

(F) practices

(G) unjust treatment

(H) prosecution

(J) belief

3 The Southern Colonies had large plantations because of the

(A) cold climate and rocky soil.

(B) lack of workers.

(C) size of the land claims.

(D) warm climate and rich soil.

4 Who founded the colony of Maryland?

(F) William Bradford

(G) James Oglethorpe

(H) Lord Baltimore

(J) John Winthrop

5 John Smith was a leader in

(A) Massachusetts.

(B) Virginia.

(C) Carolina.

(D) Plymouth.

© Pearson Scott Foresman

6 **John Winthrop led the**

(F) Pilgrims.

(G) Puritans.

(H) Separatists.

(J) dissenters.

7 **What was the official religion of the colony of Virginia?**

(A) Puritanism

(B) Quakerism

(C) Catholicism

(D) Anglicanism

8 **What did George Whitefield, Jonathan Edwards, Gilbert Tennent, and Samuel Davies have in common?**

(F) They were generals.

(G) They were founders of colonies.

(H) They were governors of royal colonies.

(J) They were preachers.

9 **What was gained from the First Great Awakening?**

(A) better relations between settlers and American Indians

(B) an increased interest in government

(C) an increased interest in religion

(D) an increased interest in moving westward

10 **What is the advantage of a free-market economy?**

(F) Certain products can be very expensive.

(G) The government does not control prices.

(H) There are no taxes on imported goods.

(J) People must pay in cash.

11 The town common in New England Colonies was

(A) the most important trading center.

(B) where people gathered for prayer services.

(C) an open space in the center where cattle and sheep could graze.

(D) a special kind of market.

12 What caused slavery to increase in the Southern Colonies?

(F) Many American Indians died.

(G) Auctions increased.

(H) Indentured servants left.

(J) Plantations grew.

13 Who were the supporters of slavery?

(A) preachers

(B) indentured servants

(C) plantation owners

(D) proprietors

14 Why did early American settlements need governments?

(F) to help solve problems and make rules

(G) to help improve relations with England

(H) to raise taxes

(J) to advise the king

15 What was the purpose of the Mayflower Compact?

(A) to ensure religious freedom

(B) to establish a basis for a government

(C) to establish the House of Burgesses

(D) to elect representatives

STOP

Name: _____

Life in the Colonies

Directions: Write the correct answer for each question in the space provided.

1 How were the English settlers self-sufficient in their new land?

_____

_____

2 Compare and contrast the land in the Southern and New England Colonies, and how the colonists used it.

_____

_____

_____

3 Why did shipping become so important in the Middle Colonies?

_____

_____

_____

4 Who were Roger Williams and William Penn?

_____

_____

_____

5 What is the difference between a proprietary colony and a royal colony?

_____

_____

_____

Name: _____

6 Why do you think people in the Middle Colonies were more tolerant of other religions?

_____

_____

7 Identify the main religious group in each of these colonies: Massachusetts, Maryland, Pennsylvania.

_____

_____

8 Describe the First Great Awakening.

_____

_____

9 How did the First Great Awakening affect religious tolerance?

_____

_____

10 What differences were there among the French, Spanish, and English colonial systems?

_____

_____

11 What role did towns play in the development of a free-market economy in the English colonies?

_____

_____

12 What is the difference between enslaved people and indentured servants?

_____

_____

13 What did enslaved people do to rebel against their situation?

_____

_____

14 Why were colonial governments not true democracies?

_____

_____

15 Explain how a person, a place, or an event shaped development in the colonies.

_____

_____

STOP

Unit 4
Answer Key

Multiple-Choice Test

1. A (H-SS 5.4.1 ELA 5RC2.4 [cause and effect])

2. G (H-SS 5.4.2; ELA 5WA1.5 [words in context])

3. D (H-SS 5.4.1)

4. H (H-SS 5.4.2)

5. B (H-SS 5.4.2)

6. G (H-SS 5.4.2)

7. D (H-SS 5.4.3)

8. J (H-SS 5.4.4)

9. C (H-SS 5.4.4)

10. G (H-SS 5.4.5)

11. C (H-SS 5.4.5)

12. J (H-SS 5.4.6; HI 3)

13. C (H-SS 5.4.6)

14. F (H-SS 5.4.7)

15. B (H-SS 5.4.7)

Short-Answer Test

1. Possible answer: Colonists grew their own food, cut down trees for shelter and warmth. (H-SS 5.4.1)

2. Southern colonies grew tobacco, rice, and indigo on large soil-rich plantations. New England colonists grew crops and raised livestock on land with rocky soil. (H-SS 5.4.1)

3. The Middle Colonies had good harbors that helped shipping grow. (H-SS 5.4.1)

4. Roger Williams was a dissenter who left Massachusetts and founded the colony of Rhode Island. William Penn established the colony of Pennsylvania. (H-SS 5.4.2)

5. An individual or group of owners controls the land in a proprietary colony. A royal colony belonged to the English monarch. (H-SS 5.4.2)

6. People from all over Europe came to settle there, so different cultures and religions learned to live side by side. (H-SS 5.4.3)

7. Massachusetts: Puritans; Maryland: Catholics; Pennsylvania: Quakers (H-SS 5.4.3)

8. It was a new way to practice the Protestant religion. It emphasized strong emotions rather than difficult ideas. (H-SS 5.4.4; ELA 5RC2.4)

9. People joined new religious groups, like the Baptists or Methodists. Some of these religions reached out to African Americans. (H-SS 5.4.4; ELA 5RC2.4)

10. The French developed trade with several American Indian groups. The Spanish focused on agriculture and used enslaved people. The English had more settlers. All of the English settlers worked either in agriculture or in various trades. (H-SS 5.4.5)

11. Towns in Middle Colonies and New England were busy trading centers. Farmers came to town to sell their crops and buy manufactured goods. (H-SS 5.4.5; HI 4)

12. Enslaved people were considered property and were bought and sold at auctions. Indentured servants agreed to work for a set period of time in exchange for housing, food, and the trip to North America. (H-SS 5.4.1 & 5.4.6)

13. They worked slowly, ran away, or bought their own freedom. (H-SS 5.4.6)

14. Only men who owned property could vote or be elected representatives. The British could pass some laws for the colonies without the colonists' consent. (H-SS 5.4.7)

15. Possible answer: The writing of the Mayflower Compact helped shape the colonies because it was the first basis of government. (H-SS 5.4.7; HI 1)

Grade 5 Teacher Module Credits

Maps
MapQuest, Inc.

Illustrations
Provided by Wilkinson Studios
Cover by Linda Helton

Photographs
Every effort has been made to secure permission and provide appropriate credit for photographic material. The publisher deeply regrets any omission and pledges to correct errors called to its attention in subsequent editions.

Unless otherwise acknowledged, all photographs are the property of Scott Foresman, a division of Pearson Education.

Photo locators denoted as follows: Top (T), Center (C), Bottom (B), Left (L), Right (R), Background (Bkgd).

Unit 3
44T5 (B) The Granger Collection, NY; 64T5 ©Gayle Ross/photo by James Fox; 64T6 (BL) ©2001, Mashantucket Pequot Museum & Research Center. All rights reserved; 64T7 (BL, BR) Marine Corps/Department of Defense

Unit 4
80T5 (BL) Brown Brothers, (BR) The Granger Collection, NY; 84T4 "The Reverend George Whitfield" England, 1768, accession # 1956-226/Colonial Williamsburg Foundation; 92T3 (BR) "Every Day's Observation" from Sketchbook of Landscapes in The State of Virginia by Lewis Miller, Virginia, ca. 1853, accession # 78.301.1/Colonial Williamsburg Foundation, (CR) "Plan of an African ship's lower deck" by Matther Carey, Philadelphia, 1797, accession # 1996-97/Colonial Williamsburg Foundation; 92T4 (BC) Medallion: "Am I Not a Man or a Brother?" by Josiah Wedgwood, Staffordshire, ca. 1790, accession # 1982-202/Colonial Williamsburg Foundation, (TR) Colonial Williamsburg Foundation; 96T5 The Granger Collection, NY

Unit 5
110T3 Prints and Photographs Division LC-USZC4-5313/Library of Congress

Unit 6
132T5 ©Frank Ore/ Stone/Getty Images

Unit 7
192T5 Library of Congress

Biography Cards
(Adams, J.) The Granger Collection, NY
(Adams, S.) The Granger Collection, NY
(Allen) Corbis
(Anthony) The Granger Collection, NY
(Arnold) The Granger Collection, NY
(Attucks) Stock Montage
(Austin) The Granger Collection, NY
(Balboa) Corbis
(Boone) Corbis
(Bradford) Pilgrim Society
(Calvert) North Wind Picture Archives

(Cartier) The Granger Collection, NY
(Champlain) ©Stock Montage/SuperStock
(Chief Logan) Ohio Historical Society
(Clark) ©National Historical Park, Independence, MO, USA/Bridgeman Art Library
(Clark) The Granger Collection, NY
(Columbus) SuperStock
(Cortes) Stock Montage Inc.
(Crockett) ©Burstein Collection/Corbis
(de Gama) Private Collection/Index/Bridgeman Art Library International Ltd.
(de Las Casas) The Granger Collection, NY
(de Soto) The Granger Collection, NY
(Dias) Private Collection/Ancient Art and Architecture Collection Ltd./Bridgeman Art Library International Ltd.
(Douglass) The Granger Collection, NY
(Duke of York) Bridgeman Art Library
(Dunmore) The Granger Collection, NY
(Edwards) Corbis
(Equiano) The Granger Collection, NY
(Franklin) ©Stock Montage/SuperStock
(Fremont) Stock Montage Inc.
(Greene) The Granger Collection, NY
(Hamilton) Stock Montage Inc.
(Hancock) Stock Montage Inc.
(Hays) ©Bettmann/Corbis
(Henry) The Granger Collection, NY
(Hooker) The Granger Collection, NY
(Houston) The Granger Collection, NY
(Hudson) The Granger Collection, NY
(Hutchinson) Bettmann/Corbis
(Jackson, A.) Getty Images
(Jefferson) ©Bernstein Collection/Corbis
(Jones) SuperStock
(Key) ©Stock Montage/SuperStock
(King Ferdinand) ©Erich Lessing/Art Resource, NY
(King George III) Giraudon/Art Resource, NY
(King, Jr.) SuperStock
(Kosciuszko) Corbis
(LaFayette) ©ARCHIV/Photo Researchers, Inc.
(LaSalle) Stock Montage Inc.
(Lewis) ©Picture History
(Madison) The Art Gallery Collection/Alamy Images
(Magellan) ©Gianni Dagli Orti/Corbis
(Marco Polo) The Granger Collection, NY
(Marion) ©Bettmann/Corbis
(Marshall) Call number Marshall, James--POR 4/©Courtesy of the Bancroft Library, University of California, Berkeley
(Marshall, J.) The Granger Collection, NY
(Mason) Corbis
(Metacom) The Granger Collection, NY
(Oglethorpe) The Granger Collection, NY
(Otis) The Granger Collection, NY
(Paine) The Granger Collection, NY
(Penn) Getty Images
(Pike) Corbis
(Pinckney) South Carolina Historical Society
(Pizarro) North Wind Pictorial Archives/Alamy Images
(Pocahontas) ©National Portrait Gallery, Smithsonian Institution/Art Resource, NY
(Polk) White House Collection, Courtesy White House Historical Association
(Ponce de Leon) The Granger Collection

(Pontiac) The Granger Collection, NY
(Powhatan) North Wind Picture Archives
(Queen Isabella) The Granger Collection, NY
(Revere) The Granger Collection, NY
(Rolfe) Detail of John Rolfe by Sidney King/©Jamestown Yorktown Foundation, Williamsburg, VA
(Ross) ©MPI/Getty Images
(Sacagawea) ©Michael Haynes
(Sampson) North Wind Picture Archives
(Santa Anna) Getty Images
(Sequoyah) ©Newberry Library, Chicago/SuperStock
(Serra) ©Lake County Museum/Corbis
(Smith, J.) The Granger Collection, NY
(Smith, Joseph) National Gallery of Art, Washington DC/SuperStock
(Squanto) Getty Images
(Stanton) The Granger Collection, NY
(Stuart) ©Robert Stuart Junior High
(Tecumseh) The Granger Collection, NY
(Tubman) ©Syracuse Newspapers/Dick Blume/The Image Works, Inc.
(Vespucci) ©Stefano Bianchetti/Corbis
(von Steuben) The Granger Collection, NY
(Warren) Corbis
(Washington, G.) The Granger Collection, NY
(Washington, M.) SuperStock
(Wheatley) Bettmann/Corbis
(Whitefield) The Granger Collection, NY
(Whitman, M.) ©Permission of The Journal of the American College of Surgeons/from *The Journal of Surgery, Gynecology and Obstetrics*/1950;50(6): 1043-1047.
(Williams) Corbis
(Winthrop) The Granger Collection, NY
(York) ©Michael Haynes
(Young) ©Underwood Photo Archives/SuperStock

Time Line Cards
(1492) SuperStock
(1513) The Granger Collection, NY
(1521) Biblioteca Nacional, Madrid
(1534) The Granger Collection, NY
(1565) North Wind Picture Archives
(1607) Jamestown National Historic Park/National Park Service/U.S. Department of the Interior
(1608) North Wind Picture Archives
(1610) Getty Images
(1620) SuperStock
(1624) The Granger Collection, NY
(1637) North Wind Picture Archives
(1664) The Granger Collection, NY
(1723) Stock Montage Inc.
(1754) The Granger Collection, NY
(1763) Bridgeman Art Library